Stacey Leigh,
5. Molne Chase
London
N.2.

455-2215.

The Love of Kittens

The Love of
Kittens

Angela Sayer

octopus

Contents

First published 1976 by
Octopus Books Limited
59 Grosvenor Street, London W1

ISBN 7064 0517 X

© 1976 Octopus Books Limited

Produced by Mandarin Publishers Limited
22A Westlands Road, Quarry Bay, Hong Kong

Printed in Hong Kong

Choosing a Kitten

All kittens are so appealing that they are often bought or adopted on impulse, but it must be remembered that kittens grow up into large and sometimes tough cats with a lifespan which averages about 14 years. Therefore, much thought should be given to the acquisition of a kitten; it will need careful, methodical feeding and rearing to adulthood, toilet training, vaccination, grooming, and adequate provision made for its welfare during holiday times. All this care will be rewarded with love and devotion, and the pleasure which comes from living with a happy pet in blooming health.

Having decided that a kitten is the right pet for you, and that its correct care will not present any major problems, it must then be determined whether it should be pedigree or pet, longhaired or shorthaired, male or female. Whatever your choice, the kitten's upkeep will cost roughly the same amount; however, it should be remembered that a poorly reared or unhealthy animal can quickly run up an enormous veterinary bill.

Attending cat shows can be a pleasant hobby, and as there are classes for neutered cats of both sexes, even if you do not intend to breed, a pedigree kitten could introduce you happily to the ranks of the Cat Fancy. Non-pedigree cats may also be shown, but there are fewer opportunities for them, and no official top awards.

A wide choice of kittens is available for the would-be purchaser, and ranges from the expensive, pedigree Persian (above) at one end of the price scale, to the appealing farmyard kittens at the other (right). The Egyptian Mau kitten (far right) would make a perfect pet for someone wanting a cat with a difference, being among the newest of breeds.

Pedigree kittens come in many varieties which are described elsewhere in this book, so there is sure to be one, at least, to appeal to any taste or preference. They are best purchased from a reputable breeder, and advertisements can be found in specialist journals, local newspapers, or by contacting breed societies. Non-pedigree kittens can be obtained from friends whose cat may have had an unwanted litter, from local farms, animal sanctuaries, or from the pet shop.

Each kitten is different and it is important to select the right kitten to fit in with your family, home and temperament. If it is at all possible, have two kittens for they will play together forever, and will provide you with more than twice the pleasure that you would get from just one. Some pedigree varieties need companionship to thrive, and cats that live in pairs always settle better in boarding catteries, or whenever they have to be left for some time. A kitten reared with a companion grows up with fewer neuroses and is easier to handle than one brought up in solitary conditions.

The points to look for when selecting a kitten are simple but important. Firstly, it is essential that the kitten be properly weaned: it should have been separated completely from its mother for at least a week before sale. Many breeders con-sider a kitten to be weaned when it starts to eat solids, forgetting how much nourish-ment it is still taking from the dam, and upon being taken to a new home, it will lose an alarming amount of weight in a very short time, solely because it is not yet capable of ingesting enough solid food to thrive. Such a setback can be fatal to a kitten, or may result in rickets or other serious defects.

Secondly, the kitten should look clean and healthy, and must be firm, without the pot-belly which could denote the presence of worm infestation. A good breeder will have ensured that the young cat has been dosed against roundworm before weaning is completed. The eyes should be bright and clear, with no sign of the third eye-lid or "haw" visible, and no discharge in the corners. Inside, the ears should be pink and moist with no tell-tale black grits in the canal which show the presence of ear-mites or "canker". The coat should be soft and clean and should be checked for flea dirts. This black grit is the flea excreta and is found around the neck, at the base of the ears and on the spine line just at the tail root. Fleas are harmful to kittens and the breeder should be prepared to clean the kitten thoroughly, if fleas are present, before it goes to a new home. A quick look at the teeth and gums to see that all is pink and healthy, and a check at the tail end to make sure that no yellow staining means that the kitten suffers from diarrhoea, and it is safe to take the little bundle home.

If possible, watch the whole litter at play before you finally choose the kitten you want. They soon settle down after your arrival, and one may even adopt you. If not, choose the kitten that appeals to you most and looks to be the most active, well-grown and healthy. If the litter is pedigree, discuss the kitten's future with the breeder, and if you are set on breeding or showing, be guided by his experience in the kitten you choose. If the kitten is to be a pet, then it does not really matter whether your preference is for a male or female, for the simple neutering operations can be carried out before puberty brings problems. However, if you are determined to breed, then the kitten you choose must be female, for only after several years of breeding experience should you keep an adult male cat, and cats do not live happily as breeding pairs.

Farmyard kittens (below right) come in all colours, and may be longhaired or shorthaired. It is important to check they are in good health like the ginger kittens (above right) before taking one home. Feral kittens (below) need a lot of veterinary attention.

Some breeders have their kittens vaccinated against Feline Panleucopenia quite early, while others feel that the vaccines are not very effective until the age of three months has passed. If the kitten has not been protected, it is advisable to get this done as soon as possible, and certainly before there is contact with any other cat. This is a good time to have the kitten checked by your veterinary surgeon, and an excellent chance to strike up a good system of regular checks for your new pet.

A pedigree kitten will have a written pedigree, a form which shows four or five generations of its ancestors, their varietal numbers and registration numbers. It will give the kitten's name, date of birth, registration number and the name and address of the breeder. A transfer of ownership form will also accompany the kitten and this is sent to the registering body with a fee to transfer the kitten officially to his new owner's name. It is very important that a pedigree kitten bought for showing or breeding should have this paperwork at the time of purchase, to save problems at a later date. Some pedigree kittens are sold as pets only, without any papers, as the breeders do not consider them to be quite up to their usual high standard of show perfection. The papers are withheld so that no unscrupulous person can buy a kitten at a greatly reduced price, just as a pet, then decide to go ahead and show or breed anyway.

Be sure to take a safe carrier with you to collect your new kitten. There are many types available, made of wicker, fibre-glass and mesh, and if you intend to show or breed it is worth investing in a really good, easily cleaned carrier, large enough for a full-grown cat, right at the beginning. If the kitten is to be a pet, then one of the collapsible, cardboard carriers will be perfectly adequate, and will serve for the few occasions when veterinary visits are necessary. A layer of newspaper topped by an old sweater will provide the comfort it needs for its journey home with you. Do not open the carrier under any circumstances, until the kitten is safely in its new home, no matter how loud the protestations from within.

On arrival home, take the kitten carefully from the carrier and make a great fuss of it. Give the run of only one room at first, having removed all possible hazards, and provide a warm cardboard box for sleeping, toilet arrangements and food and water bowls. Stick rigorously to the breeder's diet sheet for the first week at least, to prevent tummy upsets, then add new foods as you will, in tiny quantities, until accepted by the kitten. Much attention and the provision of toys, such as ping-pong balls, shuttlecocks, feathers and screwed-up paper, will help the kitten forget its littermates, and, at night, provide a well-wrapped hot water bottle and even a ticking alarm clock which will soothe and comfort the kitten's first nights without its mother.

In choosing a kitten from a non-pedigreed litter (left above), make sure that the little family has been properly weaned, and all the kittens are eating solids. If the new pet is selected from those available at an animal sanctuary, it should be carefully checked by a veterinary surgeon to ensure that it is free from parasites and any sign of infectious disease. When buying a pedigree Siamese kitten, one has the knowledge and integrity of the breeder for assurance, and the kittens will have been correctly fed, weaned and wormed before sale.

The little Lilac Points (above) are much too young to leave their mother, but the Chocolate and Lilac-Pointed kittens (left) are well grown, and quite ready to go to new homes. (Overleaf) It can be exciting to purchase one of the new varieties of foreign shorthair, such as these enchanting Egyptian Mau kittens.

Persian Kittens

Persian, or longhaired kittens, are delightful to own, and each variety has unique minor traits which make it perfect for some household. They do, however, need grooming right through, every single day, to keep the long, flowing coats free from tangles which may eventually form into dense mats. Therefore, anyone considering the purchase of a Persian kitten must be prepared to undertake regular brushing and grooming routines. Although the coat in the very young Persian is too short to tangle up easily, it is important to establish the grooming sessions early, so that they are not resented later on. For showing, Persian kittens may also need bathing, especially if they are of the lighter colour breeds. Therefore, in choosing a show specimen it is important that full consideration is given to temperament, as well as to health and beauty.

Longhaired cats were first introduced to Europe in the sixteenth century, having come from Ankara, then called Angora, in Turkey. They were mainly white and had puckish, longnosed faces with pricked ears and fine silky hair which was very long and fell in abundance from a parting along the spine. Later, broader-faced, stocky longhairs were brought from Persia, now Iran, and from matings between these two types of unusual cat came the many colours known as the Persians of today.

During the last years of the nineteenth century, Cat Shows began, and owners of unusual cats began to keep careful breeding records. Thus the first pedigrees came into existence. Various breeding groups formed and clubs and societies drew up rules and regulations and so the Cat Fancy began. Breeders decided upon standards of perfection for their own favourite breeds, and today, these Standards of Points are the criteria by which

all pedigree cats are judged for show awards.

In the Persian breeds, each variety has its own standard of points, and each desired feature is allotted a number of points, the whole adding up to 100 points in a perfect specimen. For example in the Black Persian, 25 points are given for soundness of colour, very difficult to achieve to perfection, 20 points each for coat, body structure and head, and 15 points for eyes.

The standards are worked out by the society catering for each particular breed or variety, and points are allocated in accordance with any feature needing improvement or emphasis. In Black Persians, the colour, being so difficult to produce, is given a high score, and the eyes which are usually good in any case, are given a lower score. In Blue Persians, the massive head is considered to be most important and has 25 points, and the tail receives 10.

Basically, all Persians must conform to the same general standard. The head must be large, broad and rounded, topped by tiny, wide-set, tufted ears. The cheeks are full and round and the nose is short and broad. The large, lustrous round eyes are a feature of each variety, and must conform to the desired colour. The short, stocky body has short sturdy legs and the tail, usually known as the "brush", is also very short and full, and must be free from defects such as kinks. The extra long soft fur around the neck is known as the "ruff" and is brushed up around the face for showing. Most important of all, the long dense coat must be soft and silky, never woolly, or harsh in texture, and the colour must be sound to the roots.

Obviously, not all Persians reach perfection in all characteristics, but some do

There are many varieties of pedigree
Persians, differing in coat colour and
pattern, but similar in type and conformation.
Three of the varieties are seen here:
(left) a bonny Blue Colourpoint, (above) a
Tortoiseshell-and-White, with
a striking blaze, and (top) a popular choice,
the Cream Persian.

approach the standard and become famous Champions when adult. A Persian does not have to be a Champion, though, in order to be a perfect pet.

In Britain, Longhaired kittens were, until very recent times, allowed to be shown from the age of two calendar months. This has now been changed, and the minimum age is three calendar months, while in the U.S. they must not be shown under four months. In Britain a kitten becomes an adult cat officially at nine months, while in the U.S. it will be classed as adult at eight months, which causes some confusion in deciding "When is a kitten not a kitten?"

If of the same colour all over, Persian kittens are known as Self-Coloured in Britain and as Solid-Colored in the U.S., and these varieties are usually known by their colour in their official names. There are Black, Blue, Red, Cream and White Persians in the Self-Colours, and all are very similar in their massive build and very good type and conformation. The Black is, of course, jet black, a real witches' cat with deep orange or copper eyes blazing from his midnight fur.

Most popular of all Longhaired kittens is the Blue Persian whose lustrous coat can be of any shade of blue, although the lighter tones are generally preferred. When very young, the kittens may have distinct tabby markings, but these usually fade as the kitten attains four or five weeks. The eyes, when open at seven to ten days, are a bright blue and take several months to change completely to the desired copper tone.

Red Persians are rare and very difficult to breed to standard, for they must not have tabby markings, and it is unusual to find a red without markings somewhere in the rich red coat. Usually excellent for type with enormous copper eyes, Red Persians often do extremely well on the show bench.

Cream Persians are now very popular, and take many top show awards. When they first appeared in litters they were called "fawn" and were considered to be sports. Eventually the Cream was recognized as a variety in its own right and a good specimen is a delight, like rich clotted cream in colour without any bars or tabby markings anywhere on the body or tail, and with deep copper eyecolour.

White Persians may be Blue-Eyed, Orange-Eyed, known as Copper-Eyed in the U.S., or Odd-Eyed, where one eye is blue and the other is orange. Blue-Eyed Whites have always been very popular

throughout the world, and possibly those first Angora cats which had blue eyes are still passing their genetic makeup through to the present day: it is recorded that the Angoras were frequently rather dull, and deaf in many instances, and this deafness persists in the Blue-Eyed White today.

Black Persians (below left) are thought by some to be the truly "lucky black cat" of myths and superstition, and are an old established breed. The mixed Cameo kittens (bottom left) are rare and still in the process of development in many countries, although they have been popular, and a recognized breed in the U.S., for some time. Bi-Colour kittens (right) may be had in any self colour, with white. Chinchillas (below) are beautiful at any age, and are the most photographed of all Persian cats.

It is important to ensure that the White kitten has good hearing and this is fairly easy to determine when choosing a kitten by making little squeaking noises from behind and watching the reaction. Blue-Eyed White kittens showing a dirty black smudge between the ears are rarely deaf, and the smudge grows out at the first moult.

Orange-Eyed White kittens are rarely deaf, and if the defect occurs in the Odd-Eyed variety, it is usually only on the side of the blue eye. White Persian kittens are usually palest pink when born, becoming like white swansdown puffs as they grow more coat. They need daily grooming, and a little extra attention to the tail area which, if allowed to become soiled, turns an unpleasant yellowish colour.

Tabby Persians are another group, and while conforming to the same basic type as the Self-Coloured, they have a distinctly etched, classic pattern on the

coat which is very complex. On the forehead a letter "M" can be seen, and around the eyes a lightly pencilled pair of spectacles, while swirls on the cheeks follow the facial contours. Looking at the kitten from above, a large butterfly shape is etched across the shoulders and two unbroken lines, known as "Lord Mayor's chains", run around the neck. Two lines run down the spine and the tail and legs are ringed.

In the Brown Tabby, the markings are densely black on a rich, tawny sable ground, while the eyes may be either hazel or copper. The Silver Tabby has black markings on a pure, pale silver ground, and in this variety, the eyes may be either hazel or green. The Red Tabby is a deep rich red with even darker markings and has copper eyes. American Cat Associations also recognize a Blue Tabby and a Cream Tabby, the former with darker blue markings on a pale blue

This very young White Persian (above) has the promising type desired in a future show specimen, with a wonderful, round, full-cheeked face and tiny, short tail.
The Sacred Cat of Burma (right), sometimes known as the Birman, is an intelligent breed, easily recognized by its white paws.

ground, and the latter with deep cream markings on a paler ground. Both have deep copper eyecolour.

Closely akin to the Silver Tabby is the aristocratic Chinchilla, almost a white cat with each hair just tipped with black. The kittens are very dark when born and have bars and shadowy rings on the tail. These gradually fade. The most arresting feature of this variety is the emerald or blue-green eyecolour, outlined with black or dark brown pigment, giving a model-girl look.

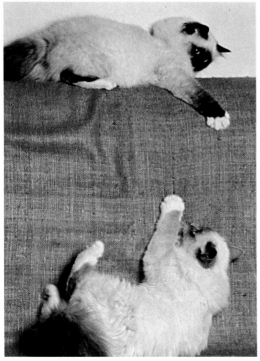

Shaded Silvers are a darker form of Chinchilla, and are recognized as a popular variety in the U.S. and other countries in the world, but not in Britain. Even breeders who are not particularly drawn towards Persian cats find the Shaded Silver to be among the most beautiful of all cats.

One shade darker still, and in the same series as the previous two varieties, is the Smoke, often called the "cat of contrasts". At first sight a Smoke kitten may be mistaken for a Black, but although the top-coat is black, the undercoat is white, and this whiteness becomes most apparent as the coat develops, forming a silvery frill. With silver ear-tufts and orange or copper eyes, Smoke Persians are among the oldest of the longhaired varieties.

An all-female variety is the Blue-Cream, a dilute form of Tortoiseshell, in which palest blue and cream colouration is present giving an ethereal, shot-silk effect.

In Britain, the standard requires the colours to be softly intermingled, while in the U.S., the colours must be patched. These kittens are always very attractive and seem to have particularly even temperaments. They are usually among top prize-winners at the shows.

Tortoiseshell Persians have patched coats of red, cream and black and have copper or deep orange eyes. They are always female, their colouration being due to a sex-linked factor, genetically, and they occur in litters where the father is red and the mother is black, or the father is black and the mother is tortoise-shell or red. There are also Tortoiseshell-and-White Persians, sometimes known as Calico Cats, which are equally patched in red, cream, black and white.

Persian cats with the Himalayan coat pattern seen in Siamese have been bred quite successfully and are known as Colourpoint Persians in Britain and as

Himalayans in the U.S. They have pale body colouring and blue eyecolour and are bred with "points", that is the extremities of the body–ears, nose, toes and tail–of different colours.

The Seal-Pointed are cream with black points, Blue-Pointed are white with deep blue points, Chocolate-Pointed are ivory with brown points, Lilac-Pointed are white with palest lilac points, Red-Pointed are white with apricot points and Tortie-Points cream with mottled points.

Very similar to the Colourpoints are the Birman, or sacred cat of Burma, but these seal and blue pointed beauties have a different bone structure to the other Persians, being longer in the head and with larger, pointed ears. The body is also longer, as is the bushy tail, and most striking of all, each foot is pure white.

One of the oldest records of cats on exhibition mentioned the Magpie, an evenly marked Black-and-White cat, and a similar variety exists today known as the Bi-Colour. Type must be the same as for other Longhaired breeds and the full coats must be evenly marked of any solid colour on white, the patches clear, and without white flecks. Eyes are deep orange or copper and any tabby markings are considered a serious fault.

Turkish cats are unlike any other Longhaired variety and were imported into Britain in 1956. They are very fond of swimming, even in cold waters, and are predominantly white with auburn markings on the face and tail. The white ears are large and upright and the Turkish has light amber eyes with pale pink rims.

Among the new varieties are several very pretty pastel-coloured Persians, bred by the mixing of the red and the silver genes. The cats are known as Cameo Persians, and may be Shell Cameo which appears as a soft pink cat, Shaded Cameo where the red tipping is heavier on the pure white base coat, or Smoke Cameo, where the coat looks red, but has a white undercoat. Cameo kittens are possibly the most fairy-like of all Persian kittens, and have delightful natures.

During the development of the Colourpoints, Self-Chocolate and Self-Lilac Persians made their appearance, and are very unusual indeed. The former has a rich chestnut coat, the latter, fur of a pale lavender tone, and both have copper eyes. When the type improves, as it will with careful breeding, these varieties will be given breed numbers and Championship status.

Some other Persians are known only in the U.S., and these include the Balinese, a longhaired cat of Siamese type, the Peke-Faced Persian, which is red and has a very flattened skull, and the unique Maine Coon cat which has been known for over 100 years.

Persian kittens make ideal pets for those who have the time to spend on daily grooming, and want a kitten that is not too demanding of attention, but is content to play quietly, and have rest periods throughout the day. Easy to rear to adulthood and devoted to his owner, the pet Persian is content to be the only cat in the household and is thus the ideal choice for the one-pet home.

Very young Persian kittens, like the Shaded Silver and the White (below), often have rather sparse coats; however, the coat length increases as the kitten grows. The unusual Red Colourpoint (right) has an excellent coat, and has been expertly groomed for his portrait session.

Shorthaired Kittens

Shorthaired varieties can be of two basic types, and in Britain the name "British" was given to those shortcoated, square and stocky cats only to distinguish them from the ones of supposedly foreign origins. The British Shorthairs are built on very similar lines to their longhaired cousins, the Persians, while the Foreign Shorthairs are their complete antithesis, being long and svelte. Colour variation and the coat patterns found in the British Shorthairs are very similar to those of the Persians, and almost identical varieties are found in the U.S., where they are known as American or Domestic Shorthairs.

The British Shorthair has a deep-chested, sturdy body, with short, stocky legs. The powerful short neck supports the massive, round, full-cheeked head with its tiny ears and large, lustrous eyes. The tail is thick at the base and fairly short and the coat is short and close, but dense to the touch.

Most British cats are known by their colour, such as British Black, Blue and so on, the Manx being unique and named after the Island of its discovery. It is also unique in being completely tailless and having a double coat. Manx cats can be of any colour or pattern and are affectionate and clownish cats to own.

Self-coloured British Shorthairs may be Black, Blue, Cream or White. The British Blue is the most popular and is a delight to own, being very affectionate but totally independent. A Blue kitten is a bundle of healthy mischief, and a good specimen with a dense, sound coat and contrasting orange eyes looks very striking.

British Blacks are difficult to breed to perfection as extremes of weather affect the coat, causing a rusty appearance. A Black in show condition, his flawless coat groomed and polished and set off by deep orange eyes, usually gathers a crowd of admirers. The coat is prepared by thorough brushing and combing, to remove all dead hair and flakes of skin, then a warmed, dry chamois leather is used to buff the coat to a mirror-like sheen.

Cream Shorthairs are comparatively rare, possibly due to the fact that they are so difficult to breed to the exacting standard which does not allow any tabby marks or bars in the pale cream coat. The exact shade of cream required is also difficult to achieve, and kittens are often produced which are of too "hot" a shade – in fact a very pale red. A good Cream is very attractive and may have either hazel or copper eyes.

As in the Persians, the White Shorthairs can have blue or orange eyes, or may be odd-eyed, and occasionally the blue-eyed variety may be deaf. Popular as models for television advertising, the amiable disposition of the White Shorthair makes it the ideal breed for this and other work calling for an even temperament. Kittens of this variety must be regularly groomed to keep them free from yellow staining, and it is usual to rub in talcum or special grooming powder, allowing it to absorb the grease, then brushing out thoroughly, leaving the coat fresh and sparkling white.

British Blue and British White shorthaired kittens meet on their first outing in the garden (above) while the older, and more adventurous British Cream (below) decides to gain the vantage point of an apple tree. (Right) Silver Tabby kittens are very striking, with dense black markings etched on a silver ground, and may have hazel or green eyecolour.

The Tabbies may be Brown, Red or Silver, and may be classic in design, mackerel in pattern, or even more exotic – spotted. The Spotted Cats are thought to be one of the oldest varieties of domestic cat, but few were seen at shows in recent years until in 1965 a few specimens once more made their appearance. Spotting may be of any shape or size, either triangular, round, rosette or star-shaped, and half of the allocated 100 points are given for the pattern, the remainder for type. Silver Spotteds have black spots on a clear silver ground; Brown Spotteds have black spots on a rich brown ground; Red Spotteds have deep red spots on an only slightly paler rich red ground. There are also Cream and Blue Spotteds and kittens of these types are very beautiful.

Classic or Marbled Tabbies must have the correct patterning if for show pur-poses. The kittens are a delight with little pansy-like faces, each etched with a large "M" on the forehead. Viewed from above the coat shows a definite butterfly shape across the shoulders. There are two "Lord Mayor's Chains" around the neck, and oyster-shaped whorls on the sides. Clearly defined spine lines and tail rings are also part of the exacting standard and there must be no sign of white hairs or a white chin. The Brown Tabby may have eyes of orange, hazel, deep yellow or green; the Red Tabby's are hazel or orange and the Silver Tabby looks best with green eyes, although hazel is permitted.

Mackerel-striped pedigree kittens are somewhat rare, especially in the Silver variety, but may be of any colouring. The markings are bold and very striking, con-sisting of many very narrow rings running vertically from the spine-line down, and the tail and chest are also clearly ringed. Many non-pedigree shorthairs have this coat pattern, which must have been selected against in the development of many of today's breeds, for it obviously ap-proximates the original "wild-type" coat.

Other British Parti-Coloured varieties include the Blue-Cream, Tortoiseshell, Tortie-and-White, and the Bi-Coloured. Tortoiseshell kittens are brightly patched with black, red and cream in equal parts and often have a striking red blaze bisecting the face between orange, copper or hazel eyes. The Tortie-and-White or Calico Shorthair has additional white patches which must not predominate, the colours being evenly distributed over the entire head, body and tail, while a white blaze is also desired, but not essential.

Blue-Cream is merely a dilution of tortoiseshell, but in this variety, the colours are preferred gently intermingled and not patched on the British show bench, while in the U.S., distinct blue and cream areas are desired. Usually of excellent type, kittens of this variety are quite irresistible, and, like the Tortoise-shell and the Tortie-and-White, are always female, due to the partial sex-linkage of the red gene in cats.

The foreign shorthaired varieties are very diverse, and each has its own special set of characteristics. The normal Abyssinian (left), with its large, tufted ears, may be shy and retiring, while the Blue Burmese (right) is normally mischievous and extrovert.

As their name suggests, Bi-Coloured Shorthairs are cats of two colours; however, the markings must not be haphazard, for the coloured areas must be clearly and evenly distributed with not more than two-thirds of the coat being coloured, and not more than one half to be white. Kittens of this variety may be of any colour with white. Early standards called for the coloured areas to be very particularly placed, in fact to be exactly as required in the Dutch rabbit, but this was impossible to achieve, and now, kittens marked attractively, one side being a near mirror-image of the other, are to be seen winning top awards at the shows.

The Foreign Shorthairs are a very diverse group, for some are derived from Siamese and are ultra-svelte, while others have precise standards of modified foreign type to which they are carefully bred. All are medium in size and shortcoated, however, and basically are long and slim in shape, with slender legs and tails, tiny paws and variously long, wedge-shaped heads with pricked ears and orientally set eyes.

Many of the "Foreigns" have, in fact, been bred in Britain to their present standard and exported all over the world, despite their evocative foreign names. The main exception to this rule is the Burmese which was developed in the U.S. and was imported to Britain in 1947. Most breeds do have some ties with the country of their title, but few reliable facts exist to trace ancestry exactly, and in any case, the judicious interbreeding and out-crossing by dedicated breeders in the past have produced the delightful foreign varieties of today, making the

present stock vastly different in total appearance to the early imports.

Recent breeding results have shown that selective principles have proved successful, for the kittens of the newer varieties are noticeably free from the defects so often apparent in their ancestors, and it is rare indeed to find crossed eyes, kinked tails and projecting sterna, and the formally common bone defects and faulty dentition have been virtually eliminated.

Abyssinian kittens have unusual coats in which each hair is ticked, rather like that of a wild rabbit. The original colour is called "normal" in Britain and "ruddy" in the U.S., and is a warm brown, shading to orange-brown underneath. The ticking consists of two or three distinct bands of colour on each hair, either black or dark brown, and this colour is also apparent on the tail tip and extending up the backs of the hind legs. The almost heart-shaped head is topped by large, expressive and often tufted, lynx-like ears, and the almond-shaped eyes may be green, yellow or hazel.

Red Abyssinians are known as Sorrel in the U.S., which is an excellent description of the exact colour. The ticking is of a deeper tone than the ground colour and the tail tip and hairs around the pads, extending up the back of the legs, are a rich brown. Nose leather and pads are pink and the eyecolour is similar to the Normal variety. Other colours are appearing in the Abyssinian series and some delightful kittens have been seen in silver, blue, cream, lilac and a dilute chocolate shade. All have been ticked with darker colours and have had the typically whimsical expression of the true Abyssinian.

Burmese kittens closely rival the Siamese nowadays in the popularity stakes. Some colours recognized in Britain are not recognized in the U.S. and in other countries, and the standards do vary on opposite sides of the Atlantic. The original Brown or Sable Burmese is a very dark and glossy brown, sometimes showing very faint "points". The coat is very short and close-lying, and the head should be less pointed than that of the Siamese. A natural dilution appeared early on, in which the Blue variety emerged. This was followed later by the arrival of some Chocolate or Champagne kittens and eventually, when cats carrying both blue and chocolate genes intermated, the elusive Lilac or Platinum variety came into being.

Scientifically designed breeding programmes were set up to introduce the red gene into Burmese, and eventually the full spectrum of Burmese coat colours was produced. Beautiful kittens have been born in the new varieties in Red,

Cream, Tortie, Chocolate-Cream, Blue-Cream and Lilac-Cream. The dilute torties are very pretty and make delightful spayed pets. Burmese kittens are easy to train, intelligent and mischievous, and get on well with other cats, and with dogs.

Havana kittens are glossily brown and have eyes which change from baby-blue to a deep lime green during their first six months. Extremely oriental in type, with extra long and lithe body, legs and tail, and a head of Siamese shape is the standard called for in Britain where this breed was manufactured in the 1950s. In the U.S., however, the early imports were bred along different lines and the Havana Brown there is a small and rather dumpy little cat with a deep stop in the profile, giving a "puppy-dog" look, although the standard for colour of coat and eyes is the same. Havana kittens should never be left alone for long periods. They are best kept as neutered pairs, or with another kitten or dog for company, for being extra-intelligent and alert, they are not at their best when deprived of companionship.

Closely related to the Havana is the ethereal Foreign Lilac, palest lavender-grey all over the svelte body, with oriental eyes of clear lime green. The Foreign Black or Ebony is another in the same Siamese-derived series, and is jet black, long and lithe. It also sports the green

eyecolour. Bred originally from Siamese cats by eradicating the gene which restricted the colour to the points, the Foreign Black is the "self" version of the Seal-Point, the Havana is the "self" Chocolate, and the Foreign Lilac is the "self" Lilac-Point.

Foreign White kittens are striking with their brilliant blue eyecolour. They are Siamese in disguise, the white merely masking the points colour. Born pure white, they stay this way throughout their lives. Carefully bred for several generations before recognition was granted, all the "self" Siamese-derived foreigns excel in health and temperament, as well as beauty, for equal importance was placed on these factors in the early selection of breeding stock during their developmental years.

The white Devon Rex kitten (opposite above) has the characteristic, pixie-like expression of the breed, and an excellent, closely-waved coat. Foreign Blacks (opposite below) known as Ebony cats in some countries, are jet black, with short, glossy coats and Siamese body structure. Korat cats (above left) are silver-blue in colour, and come from Thailand, where they are regarded as good-luck charms. The Brown Burmese kitten in the waste paper basket (above) has a shaded coat which will eventually darken to a deep, glossy brown.

Rex kittens have curled coats and there are two main types, the Devon Rex and the Cornish Rex, each caused by a distinctly separate gene. In 1950, a curly-coated kitten was found in an otherwise normal litter of kittens born on a farm in Cornwall, and a new breed was conceived. Ten years later, on another farm in Devon this time, a neighbouring county in England, another curled kitten turned up, and it was thought that it was caused by the same rex gene. Breeding tests showed that this was erroneous, and the two curly varieties of cat are bred along quite different lines.

The Cornish Rex has a long, flat-skulled head topped by high-set, large ears, the eyes being medium in size and almond in shape. In the Devon Rex, the head is full-cheeked and medium in length with a distinct whisker break and a short muzzle. The almond-shaped eyes are larger than in the Cornish and the ears are set much lower on the head. Both should have dense, very short fine coats, forming waves over the entire body and even the whiskers and eyebrows should be curled.

Russian Blue kittens have softly smiling faces and the most loving of temperaments. It is said that they descend from cats brought to Britain from Archangel in the nineteenth century; however, the blue colour is due to a simple dilution of black,

known as the Maltese factor, and blue cats have appeared all over the world for centuries. Quiet-voiced and gentle, Russian Blues are charming and quite content to be the only pet in a loving family. The short, close coat should have an unusual texture like sealskin, and is of a silvery slate-blue colour. The medium wedge head is topped by rather upright pricked ears, and the eyes should be of a decided green shade.

Bred only in Thailand and then in the U.S. for many years, another blue foreign cat is the Korat, the Thai symbol of good luck and fortune. Now also bred in Britain, this rather unique cat has a silver-blue coat and rather full eyes of an unusual bright green-gold. The heartshaped face is accentuated by the ear placement, and the overall effect is of a shy smallish cat of intermediate type.

An exciting Siamese-derived variety is the re-creation of the ancient cat of the Pharaohs, called in Britain the Egyptian Mau by those working on its development as a special breed. The Mau is a pale bronze in colour and has large spots of a deep, rich brown scattered over the whole of the body. The long, wedge-shaped head is strikingly etched in the same bronze tones and the mark of a scarab beetle is clearly defined between the very large pricked ears. The full but oriental-shaped

eyes are a bright, clear apple green. This variety is known as the Bronze Mau, and other shades have also turned up in various litters. Silver Mau have black spots on a clear silver ground; Lilac Mau are lavender-spotted on a mushroom ground; Blue Mau have slate spots on a silvery blue ground and Sable Mau have black spots on a warm fawn ground.

Breeders of foreign shorthairs are always bringing recessive genes to the surface and producing new colour combinations. Combining the normal colours and patterns with the silver genes has added a vast new spectrum of possible colourations to the Cat Fancy. Foreign Shorthairs are basically very similar, however, whatever colour their overcoat might be, and make adorable and devoted pets.

In producing new varieties, careful crosses are made by experienced breeders, selecting genetic features desired in the proposed breed. This famous litter from a Chocolate-tabby-point Siamese father, and a Havana mother, was planned as both parents carried the blue dilution gene. As expected, foreign Lilac kittens were born, plus a Havana, a Chocolate-pointed Siamese and the added bonus of bronze and lilac Egyptian Mau. The bronze Mau (right) is the grandson of the lilac Mau just disappearing at the rear of the litter.

Siamese Kittens

Unique among kittens are the vocal, faithful clowns, the Siamese. Due to a mutation which caused the colour of the coat to be restricted to the areas known as the "points", that is the muzzle, ears, legs and tail, this unusual pattern, known as the Himalayan factor, is also found in other domestic animals, such as mice and rabbits. This factor is also connected with the production of the fantastic blue eye-colour which has done so much to make the Siamese the most popular of all breeds of cat throughout the world.

Originally imported to Britain from Siam, now Thailand, at the end of the nineteenth century, the first Siamese cats were frail, exotic creatures. Treated somewhat like hot-house plants, and fed on strange diets, they often became sick and died. It says much for the tenacity of the breed that from such daunting beginnings it has achieved the numbers and diversity of colour varieties that we see today.

Siamese kittens are born pure white and the queen usually has about five in the litter. The eyes open from three days onwards, much earlier than in Longhaired or British Shorthaired breeds, and must be protected from too much light at this stage. As the days go by the points begin gradually to colour up, and are quite distinct by the time the kittens are toddling out of the maternity box at four weeks. At ten weeks of age the eyes have changed from baby-blue to a true Siamese blue, but will probably not have reached full intensity at that stage. In a mixed litter it is not always possible, even for an experienced breeder, to recognize all the colours until the kitten has reached the age of three months, and the pads under the paws are usually the best indication of what the adult colour will be.

The original Siamese were Seal-Points. This is the effect of the Himalayan factor on a shorthaired black cat. The black colouring is restricted to the extremities of the body, and is given a slightly paler appearance, known as Seal-Brown. The coat, white in kittenhood, gradually becomes a warm buff, shading to fawn on the flanks as the kitten matures, and the mask, or muzzle, dark up to the eyeline at first, gradually extends towards the forehead, connecting with fine tracings from the eyebrows to the black ears at the age of nine months.

As we have previously seen in the Shorthairs, a simple dilution, the Maltese factor, causes black to appear as blue, and this happened spontaneously in Siamese cats also. Kittens appeared with paler points and these were called Blue-Points. Blue-Pointed Siamese have the same characteristics as the Seal-Points. The body is very pale in a good specimen and of a cold tone, and the points are of an attractive slate-grey colour. The pads of the feet are a dark blue colour as compared to black in the Seal-Points, and clear, bright vivid blue eyes are desired.

In the early imports from Siam, the recessive chocolate gene must have lurked, for in some litters, kittens with paler points were born through the years. Most were discarded as being "poor" specimens, in favour of the more striking Seal-Points, but eventually, these Chocolate-Points were recognized as a separate variety and were developed as such. Chocolate-Pointed Siamese have ivory bodies which stay pale throughout their lives. The points are the colour of milk chocolate, and in a good specimen, all the points will match exactly. In most kittens of this variety, however, the ears and tail are dark, the mask slightly paler and the legs hardly coloured at all. This usually improves with age, but Chocolate-Points are slow to mature colourwise.

By far the most popular of all the Siamese varieties is the Seal-Pointed, originally known as the Royal Cat of Siam (above). Siamese kittens are all born white, whatever their eventual points colour, and this captivating kitten (right) is just acquiring the slate-blue tipping which indicates that it will be a Blue-Point.

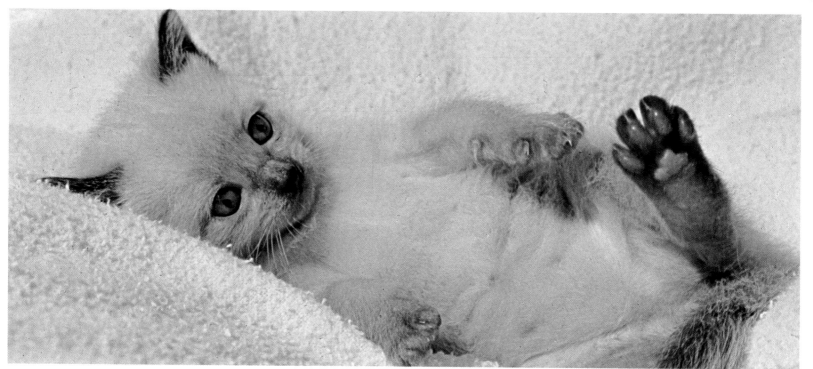

Lilac-Pointed Siamese (above left) occurred naturally, when cats carrying both chocolate and blue genes were intermated, and when compared with the Blue-Pointed Siamese (above right) can be seen to be distinctly paler in both body and points colouration. The Tabby-Pointed Siamese (left) is a striking example of a man-made variety.

Eventually, with the development of Blue-Points and Chocolate-Points, as well as the favourite Seal-Pointed Siamese, cats which carried both blue and chocolate genes were intermated. When this happened the elusive Lilac-Points emerged. At first they were thought to be very pale and therefore very poor Blue-Points, but eventually it was realized that a new variety had arisen, and steps were taken to obtain recognition and a standard of points. Lilac-Pointed Siamese are white, with delicate, dove-grey points.

They have soft voices to match their colouring and are very gentle, loving creatures.

Experimental breeders decided to introduce other factors into the Siamese breed, and this was not undertaken lightly, for it is expensive and time-consuming to raise the necessary number of litters to create a new variety and to bring it to recognition point. The factors to be introduced were the red gene and the tabby gene. Matings were made between Siamese Seal-Points and red cats and over the years, with very careful selection and backcrosses to the best Siamese stock, some delightful new varieties came forth. We have the Red-Point Siamese, elegant and striking with a white coat and bright apricot points. A dilute cousin is the Cream-Point with his white coat finished off by points which can best be described as a colour somewhere between thick Devon cream and pale sand. The female

equivalents of these two varieties, although it must be stated that we do have female Red- and Cream-Pointed Siamese also, are the various Tortie-Points.

Seal Tortie-Points have points which are speckled black, red and cream; Chocolate Tortie-Points have their extremities peppered with chocolate and cream; Blue Tortie-Points are pointed in blue and cream and Lilac Tortie-Points have points ethereally mingled in lilac and palest cream. The Tortie-Points are often looked upon with distaste by judges, but no two are ever alike and for those who want a kitten that is completely unique, a Tortie-Point Siamese, perhaps with a bizarre blaze, makes a really unusual pet. It is an interesting brood queen if to be bred from, for she will have most gloriously mixed litters, depending upon the sire used.

The introduction of the tabby factor into Siamese was condemned by all the purest breeders, who were sure that "ordinary" Siamese would be ruined by such a disastrous and retrograde step. As it transpired, the Tabby-Points are among the most typical of all Siamese, and Seal-Points bred from them have won top show honours all over the world. In Tabby-Pointed Siamese, the body should be pale and unmarked, although some ghost tabby markings do appear as the cat grows older. The points have strongly etched tabby markings across the cheeks and the legs and tail are strikingly ringed. The ears have marks like large thumb-prints on the backs, and the lips are speckled.

Tabby-Points may be Seal, Chocolate, Blue or Lilac and even Red Tabby-Point and Cream Tabby-Point, although these are virtually impossible to tell from the Red-Point and Cream-Point which often show ghost striping. In the Seal and the Blue, the coats do tend to become rather patterned with age, but the Chocolate Tabby-Point keeps his ivory coat and his lovely bronze-toned striped points through life. The Lilac Tabby-Point also stays very pale, and is a very pleasing cat to own, although rather rare and difficult to acquire.

Whatever their points colour, or pattern, Siamese must all conform to the same standard of points. Everything about a Siamese should be long and slender – body, neck, legs and tail. The head is long and narrow and forms a wedge shape, the large, open and pricked ears continuing the lines of the face giving a "marten" look. The eyes are always distinctly blue and oriental in shape and setting. They must not be crossed in a squint, which is considered a bad fault in the breed. The long tail should taper to a point and must not be kinked. Originally, many Siamese had kinked tails, but this has been largely bred out now.

Siamese kittens are really delightful to own, and should preferably be kept in twos, when, if neutered and well reared, they will play together for the whole of their life span. If kept alone, a Siamese kitten must be given a surfeit of love and attention and many toys to keep him amused and to develop his full intelligence. They are ideal for folks who live in apartments, or houses without gardens, and happily adapt to a life spent entirely in the safety of the home.

The Tabby-Pointed Siamese (below) is of the blue variety, and the elegant fellow (right) is a Red-Point Siamese.

Caring for the New Kitten

Once you have decided upon your new kitten, it is up to you to provide a suitable home for it, and to rear it to healthy adulthood. Before going to collect the kitten, it is advisable to have a few things ready. Firstly, only one room should be available for exploration during the first few days. Then, as the kitten learns the whereabouts of such important items as his toilet tray, he can be given more freedom in the house.

Make sure that there are no chimneys that he can climb, no electric cord that he might bite through, no unguarded fire into which his tail can swing and become singed, and that there are no access holes into the backs of stoves, refrigerators and freezers, for kittens can and do crawl into the tiniest spaces, and can be very difficult to extract. There must be no open windows or doors when he first arrives, for even the most placid of kittens may be very upset and alarmed during his first journey into strange surroundings.

The main essentials for comfort are firstly a small cardboard box for bedding, with several layers of newspaper for warmth, topped by an old sweater. Do not buy fancy baskets at this stage for the kitten may be dirty in his bed at first, and wickerwork is extremely hard to clean efficiently. Newspapers, sweater and box can be burned when they are soiled, and replaced.

Secondly, have ready a shallow toilet tray with suitable litter, preferably the same litter as used by his breeder. This should be conveniently placed on a large sheet of newspaper, not too far from his bed, and he can be shown it at intervals until he has once used it. After that he will remember its whereabouts. This tray must be regularly changed and not allowed to become soiled or offensive, for

The little Foreign Black (top left) explores a large jug, while the British Cream (centre left) has climbed to a precarious perch on the dresser. Most kittens will come readily when mealtimes draw near (bottom left). Above: children must be shown how to handle small kittens correctly.

then the kitten will refuse to use it and might become dirty in his habits.

A spill-proof bowl for drinking water is essential and should not be too deep, for the kitten is still learning to lap at this stage and a deep bowl will force his nose into the liquid at the wrong angle, causing him to splutter and possibly putting him off drinking his water ration daily. The water must be changed every day and the bowl washed out. If detergent is used it must be thoroughly rinsed away as traces left behind can cause gastric problems.

Feeding dishes can be of any material, china, glass or plastic, but must be free from cracks and easy to clean. Again, a shallow dish is easier for a small kitten to manage, and food should be arranged in little peaks at first until he really gets the idea of licking the platter clean.

Finally, some sort of carrier is necessary for carrying your new kitten home. Obviously a proper container is the best, but it is not essential, for a disposable cardboard carrier obtainable from the pet-shop or veterinary surgery will do. Failing this, any zip-top bag can be used, but it is important to close the zipper completely once the kitten is safely inside. If his nose can peep out, the whole kitten can swiftly follow, and many young animals have been lost on buses and trains through mistaken kindness in half-opening the zipper or lid of the carrier. Keep it safely closed until you are home. If the weather is cold, a hot-water bottle

wrapped in old sweaters may be placed in the carrier, and if a wickerwork basket is used, wrap several layers of brown paper around the outside, securing this with sticky tape to make it draughtproof.

When you and your kitten are safely home, take him gently from the carrier and put him in his bed. Make sure all other pets are out of the room, and any humans are sitting down quietly. He will soon get his bearings and start to explore nervously. Make much of him from time to time, and when he has had a look around, offer his favourite food from his diet sheet.

At bedtime, you may feel guilt pangs and want to take the kitten to bed with you, but please do not. It is not good for him, and it will not be good for you when he is fully grown and has appropriated your pillow. Make sure he knows where his tray is, put down fresh food and water and, if the weather is cold, put a well-

wrapped hot water bottle in his box and place him on it. It must not be too full or the kitten cannot snuggle into the warmth. You must remember that you are trying to make up for the loss of his mother, so he needs a warm, soft something to cuddle up to. If he howls, you could try putting a ticking clock near his bed. This is very soothing to a small kitten, possibly because it approximates a heartbeat.

The breeder should provide a diet sheet and this should be carefully read for content and quantities of food. Most folks give new kittens much too much of the wrong things when they first acquire them, and end up with a poor little cat with gastritis. If the breeder says "No milk", then please do not give milk; it could be that this particular strain has an intolerance to milk products. If you feel that you want to feed some things which are not on the chart, then wait for a week or so to introduce the new foods gradually. If the kitten gets chronic diarrhoea, stop the new food at once.

Make sure your kitten has plenty of play opportunity at this stage, for his behaviour patterns are being formed and the more enriched his environment during early kittenhood, the more intelligent and amusing he will be as an adult cat. Cardboard boxes and paper bags make wonderful kitten-sized caves, and pipe-cleaner spiders, cat-nip mice, ping-pong balls and small woolly toys are most acceptable. Plastic hair rollers seem to be a great favourite with Siamese, and will be tossed about for hours. Some kittens are aspiring football stars for they will dribble a ball up and down a smooth floor using both forepaws with equal panache.

Regular grooming is vital to the well-being of any kitten and should be started very young, especially if he is longhaired when a daily brush and comb right through from head to tail is essential. Short-haired British cats need carefully combing daily, for the coat is thick and as it grows the dead undercoat can be retained. Then, if swallowed during the kitten's normal lick-and-promise grooming routine, it may give rise to a hair-ball in the stomach. This thick wad of hair may require an operation in order to remove it. Foreign Shorthairs need only grooming with the hand, firm strokes from head to tail tip, to remove dead hair and to give a gleam to the coat.

To groom a Persian kitten, a fairly stiff but not too harsh a brush is used and the fur is gently teased through over the whole body. A broad-toothed metal comb is used to tease out any tangles and powder can be sprinkled into the coat to remove grease or stains, then brushed out. Finally the kitten is brushed through the "wrong"

way from tail to head. The tail is given a shake from the tip to separate all the hairs and the ruff is brushed up to frame the face.

British Shorthairs are combed with a fine-toothed metal comb. This removes any dead or loose hair and cleans the coat of dust particles. A soft, dry chamois leather, a pad of cotton wool or an old silk scarf can then be used to buff the coat and to tone the muscles. These kittens like quite firm treatment and can be buffed fairly hard once they are old enough to have a good muscle layer.

Foreign Shorthairs can be combed with a fine-toothed comb also, then brushed with a fairly soft bristle brush. They are finally buffed in the same way as the British, but then usually go and roll in the very dustiest part of the garden they can find, especially if they are pale-coated Siamese!

*Persian kittens must be groomed daily
from a very early age, to keep the coat
in good condition and prevent tangling (above
left). Not as lively or mischievous as
the shorthaired breeds, they are, however,
like all kittens, highly inquisitive.
This kitten (below) scratching at his head,
should be carefully checked for fleas
or mites deep in the ear canal.*

Once a week the ears, teeth and claws should be inspected. The ear of the cat is the perfect niche for a rather nasty little mite which lives in the canal, causes great irritation and distress to the cat, and gives rise to the condition often called "canker". The presence of this mite is detected by dark-brown grits in the ear canal and if seen should be shown to the veterinary surgeon without fail. Kittens often get very grubby ears, for the natural appearance of the inner ear flap is pink and moist and covered with a thin grease layer. In young kittens, rolling and playing in the dust, dirt particles often stick to this waxy layer and form dark clumps. These are best wiped away with dry cotton earbuds.

The teeth are very important, for if the mouth is sore the kitten will stop eating and rapidly lose condition. The milk teeth are shed gradually throughout the first few months to be replaced by the permanent teeth, and sometimes the second teeth come through while the first teeth are still present. This double dentition is easy to detect, and a kindly owner will check weekly to make sure the whole mouth is healthy, taking any problems to the veterinary surgeon.

Kittens have three eyelids, the normal two which we all have, plus a special one, often called the "haw" which crosses the eye from the inside corner outwards. If a

kitten is unwell, running a temperature, has a worm infestation or is having teething problems, chances are that the "haw" will show as a sort of skin in the corner of the eye. If the haw shows, it usually means some sort of trouble, and if the kitten has not had any unusual food, or a pill, then a visit to the veterinary surgeon is called for. Soreness of the rims is often caused by a smokey atmosphere or dust, and bathing the eyes with a saline solution is quite in order, as long as it is sterile and the cotton-wool is only used once, then discarded. No ointments should be put in kittens' eyes unless on veterinary advice.

Claw-stropping can be a great nuisance in cats kept entirely indoors, for even if provided with scratching blocks, some kittens, notably Siamese, seem to delight in shredding carpets and covers. It is very important to stop this while the kitten is tiny and does not do much damage at each session. When he is grown and weighs 10 or 12 pounds it will not be amusing. Claws may be trimmed with proper clippers; scissors must never be used as they will split the claws, and the veterinary surgeon will show you how it should be done. The kitten will still strop after claw trimming but will not do so much damage. A proper board or carpet-covered log should be provided for house-bound cats and can be impregnated with cat-nip. Every time stropping commences, place the kitten on the board or log and make much of him. He will learn.

During the grooming session, inspection of the coat for parasites is obvious, although kittens kept solely indoors will be very unlikely to harbour such things as fleas and lice. Flea excreta show in the fur as tiny black grits. If these are present,

then you will eventually find a flea or two. The fine-toothed comb is ideal and will neatly lift the insect from the fur when it should be rapidly destroyed before it has a chance to jump away. Dipping the comb into a small pot of disinfectant is effective, or, for the less squeamish, the application of a firm thumb does the trick just as well.

If the new kitten is to go outside unaccompanied as he grows older, his toilet tray can be gradually moved to the garden until he learns just where it is required that he should go. He also may wear an elasticated collar bearing his name and address in case he gets lost or strays. Care should be taken, though, that the collar is made for cats and fits correctly, for if a puppy collar is used and the kitten should get caught on a branch or twig, he may be hanged. With a proper cat-collar correctly fitted, the elastic inserts give sufficiently in such an emergency to enable the head to slip out and the animal can escape to safety.

For taking a kitten on holiday or in the car, a special harness and lead may be purchased, and it is quite simple to fit; most cats take to it well if started in early kittenhood. No cat will learn to walk on the lead to heel as a dog does, this being far beneath their dignity, but it is a means of controlling a cat or kitten in a situation where escape is possible, without confining it to a carrier. Collars and harnesses should never be left on the kitten for long periods as the friction caused by natural movement will cause rubbing on the coat at contact points, and will cause the hair to mark, sometimes quite severely.

Introducing the new kitten to an established family pet can be a traumatic experience for all concerned, and must be undertaken in a carefully planned,

methodical way. The new kitten must be allowed to settle in the home for a couple of days or so to get his bearings and to become relaxed before he sees the other cat or dog. To introduce two felines, the older pet should be allowed to enter the room in which the new kitten has settled. It will usually enter, then become aware of the new kitten's scent and show signs of aggression. The kitten will probably bounce out at the cat, turn slightly sideways and fluff up. Both may hiss alarmingly at one another. This may well continue for up to a week, or they may make friends very quickly. In any case, do not leave the two alone without supervision, and do not expect them to share a food bowl; this is just asking for trouble.

Dogs are introduced to the new kitten in the same way, usually being kept on a lead and being allowed to get just within sniffing distance of the kitten. Much fuss must be made of the dog and he must be reassured all the time that this is a friendly kitten and that he is a very good dog! Again, the two should not be left alone at first, but, unless the dog really dislikes cats, or has been very spoiled, they should soon become firm friends.

Children and kittens can become good friends, the important thing being that each has respect for the other. Even tiny babies can be taught that to feel a kitten's coat is pleasurable, and the flat of the child's hand can be gently passed across the fur of the animal. Babies taught in this way never grab at or squeeze any animal. Older children should be taught that the kitten must not be lifted high or he may jump down and break his legs. He must not be squeezed or have his head, legs or tail pulled. He likes gentle games but must have lots of sleep and rest periods. They must also be taught to wash their hands after playing with the kitten.

Most children get along well with young cats and enjoy learning how to hold and carry them correctly, to brush and comb them and to shake out the bedding daily, and the kitten can teach much to the children with regard to the establishment of a respectful relationship. Kittens are not playthings, however, and should not be dressed in dolls' clothes or wheeled in the dolls' carriage although they may enjoy such games when older and stronger.

Kittens love to climb and the exercise is good for developing the muscles, and for keeping the claws trim.

When tiny, the forcing of head and legs into tiny garments can do untold harm, and the kitten may jump, frightened, from the moving carriage.

No matter how much love, grooming and warmth the new kitten receives, he will not do well unless he is fed an adequate diet. Although the breeder's diet sheet must be adhered to firmly at first, changes may be made as the kitten settles in the new home, for some items may be difficult to obtain in small quantities or in your neighbourhood, or may be inconvenient for you to prepare.

Water is the first requirement as already mentioned, and must be fresh each day. The kitten needs a lot of proteins, which are found in meat, fish, offal and cheese, fats from meat, and a selection of vitamins and mineral salts. In the wild, a kitten would eat prey brought by its mother. First the entrails containing part-digested vegetable matter would be eaten, then the rest of the carcass including all the fur or feathers and the bones. It is not suggested that you catch prey for your kitten, but do try to remember what it is that you are trying to replace in his diet. A sensible way to feed a small kitten is to give four meals a day until he is six months old, then three meals until he is nine months and just about full-grown. Then he can have a morning snack and a large main evening meal for the rest of his life.

Meat—cooked, raw, tinned or dried—should form the bulk of your pet's diet. Any sort of meat will do, but do not feed one sort all the time. Liver, once or twice a week, will make sure that your kitten gets sufficient Vitamin A which is vital to his well-being. Fish is enjoyed but again should be given only once or twice a week. The excellent canned foods are enjoyed by most cats, but care should be taken to see that they are all meat and not bulked out with carbohydrates. Prepacked meats made for dogs, and with a special ingredient to ensure that they have a long shelf-life, must not be given to cats as the preservatives could be toxic. Complete dried diet foods are available, but controversy has raged as to whether the feeding of these could cause kidney problems. These foods are well-balanced and would seem perfectly safe as long as the kitten is drinking plenty of water.

Most kittens enjoy chewing bones and this activity helps with teething and promotes healthy gums. Large strips of raw meat are also excellent for this purpose and if one meal daily can consist of a strip of raw meat so much the better. The breeder's diet sheet might possibly suggest giving two milk and cereal feeds daily too, but you may find that once you have your kitten home he immediately decides that he will give up such habits and become carnivorous.

Only butcher's meat should be fed to your kitten and if fish, rabbit and chicken is cooked, it should be stewed or baked thoroughly and allowed to cool, and all skin and bones must be removed before offering to the kitten. Food must not be fed straight from the refrigerator, nor must it be too hot. Room temperature is best and prevents gastric upset.

It is not necessary to give lots of vitamin pills to your kitten, but a calcium-with-Vitamin-D tablet daily while he is growing is quite a good idea, and some brewer's yeast tablets from time to time will keep him very perky. After illness, the veterinary surgeon will possibly advise a course of vitamins, but a healthy kitten having a good, well-balanced and sensible diet will obtain all he needs from his food.

Contrary to popular belief, cats and dogs are not natural enemies, and the new kitten, missing his littermates, will appreciate the attentions of a friendly canine.
The newly acquired kitten needs a great deal of rest, between periods of play, and will settle down happily in a blanket-lined basket.

Having Kittens

As your kitten grows up you may wonder whether or not to have it neutered. If it is a male, you really have no choice, for as an entire male matures, the odour of his urine changes dramatically and becomes most unpleasant. The cat begins to "spray" or to mark his territory out with carefully placed, fine jets of spray, and he will not restrict his marking to the garden. The curtains, covers and carpets will all receive their mark, and will eventually begin to smell extremely bad. The entire tom will also roam to seek lady friends and in doing so will have to fight with other males when crossing their territory. He may not always come off the best and large veterinary bills can accrue for treatment of torn and abcessed ears, broken claws and lacerated legs. Bites in the tail base are also common and abcess freely, taking a long while to clear up.

Neutering of the male kitten at about six to seven months presents no problems and is performed under a general anaesthetic. By this age the kitten has laid down the foundations of firm masculine muscle and is not so likely to get fat and lazy as a kitten neutered at three or four months. He is also less likely to get urinary problems in later life if neutered rather late in kittenhood. Very few kittens have any adverse after-effects from the simple operation, and soon settle down to become perfect pets.

It is important not to overfeed any cat, but the neutered male is particularly prone to overweight and his diet must be carefully watched at all times. It should be varied and not include much fish which might give rise to skin problems. A chunk of raw meat each day is excellent and will help to keep teeth and gums in good condition; a little fat of some kind will help the skin; and some cat biscuits or complete diet food will provide all the essential nutrients he needs. Fresh cold drinking water must, or course, always be readily available.

A female kitten can be neutered at any age after about 12 weeks, but it is better to let her mature to a certain extent first. Many people like their kitten to have a litter of her own before being spayed, as the operation is called, but it is easier for the surgeon, and less serious for the cat, if performed before she has had a period of heat or oestrus. As in the male kitten, the operation is performed under a general anaesthetic, and in the U.S., the incision is usually made midline, that is from the navel and back about an inch. In Britain and other countries, the incision is made through the flank. The site must be shaved, and later stitched, and takes about one week to heal before the stitches may be removed. The hair grows back in a few weeks, leaving no trace of the scar, except in Siamese cats where the hair may grow dark until the first moult.

The kitten is usually allowed to return home within a few hours of the operation, but may be sleepy and still suffering from the anaesthetic until the following morning. She should be kept quietly in her carrier until her reactions are back to normal, and should not be handled while still unsteady, or she may bite or claw you. Some kittens bite at the stitches and may succeed in removing them. If this happens, the veterinary surgeon should be contacted at once for advice.

If your female kitten is pedigreed and you bought her for her show potential and good looks, then possibly you have already decided to try breeding from her. Her first heat will probably occur at about nine months of age, but it could be earlier and may be much later; there are no hard and fast rules for sexual maturity in the cat. The first heat is usually fairly brief, and the kitten must be kept closely confined and not allowed out of doors until all signs have diminished. The second heat follows after only a few weeks, and if the kitten is virtually mature she may be mated.

Well before this, the stud cat should have been selected. The breeder of your female will be able to tell you about suitable stud males, not too far from your home. The owner is contacted and arrangements made for your female to be taken when she comes into season. The fee is discussed, and the pedigree of your female read to the stud's owner.

For a maiden female it is best to use the services of an experienced stud cat and he should be a good example of his breed, excelling in the show points in which your kitten is weak. If she has a poor tail, his should be extra good and so on. The owner will be an experienced breeder and sure to be able to give excellent help and advice.

Most pedigree queens, as female cats are known, make excellent mothers and are devoted to their offspring, as may be seen in the Abyssinian (above) and the Red Burmese (right), patiently enduring the attentions of their kittens.

Having made the arrangements well in advance, the stud owner must be contacted on the first day of the female's heat. It is usual then to take the female safely in her carrier to the stud owner's home on the second day, when she will be put into a special pen in the stud house to get to know the male without actually being able to contact him. She will be very vicious and hiss and snarl at him for several hours before being ready to mate, and this usually takes place on the third day and is supervised by the stud owner.

Several matings will take place over the next day or so, and then the owner of the male will ask that the little female, or queen as she may now be known, be collected.

Safely home again, the female must be kept closely confined, for she may still be in season, and fed a light diet and given much attention to settle her down. If she has conceived, she will look slightly bulgy in about three weeks after mating, and the full gestation period is 65 days.

If the female has not conceived, then she should "call" or come on heat again in about three weeks after the unfruitful mating. Most stud owners will give a free return mating in such a case, but they are not obliged to, for it is up to the owner of the female to present her at the right time for conception. In the cat, ovulation takes place when stimulated by the act of mating. Some owners take their queens too early in the heat, and some too late. Some queens are so spoiled and humanized that they have forgotten that they are cats, and so refuse to mate at all.

To the stud owner, the best sort of maiden queen to have belongs to a sensible person who has read all the right cat books and has raised her little female to eat a good all-round diet, to like other humans and other cats, and is well balanced in mind and body. This sort of female will settle down with the minimum of fuss and not do the precious stud cat any damage. She will eventually mate up, allow herself to be handled, eat her supper and return home safely pregnant. This sort of queen also proves to have an easier parturition and is a good mother.

Once the female looks safely pregnant, her rations may be very slightly increased and extra calcium can be added to her diet. About one week before the birth, a large box should be provided in some suitable warm, dimly lighted, airy place.

The pregnant queen spends much of her time relaxing in the sunshine, while her litter develops. Once the kittens are born her reserves of calcium may be quickly depleted by lactation, unless she is fed a well-balanced diet.

It should have quite a stack of newspapers tossed in and a convenient hole made in the side just large enough for the mother-to-be to get through. A loose cardboard top can be made so that you can look in to watch progress. For the last few days before the birth, the queen will pace all over the house looking in all sorts of unsuitable spots and returning to her box now and again to tear up the newspapers into a nest. A few hours before the birth the teats become very enlarged and she will refuse her food. Her voice may change its tone and she may be very restless and not sure what to do.

It is a good idea to warn your veterinary surgeon of the impending birth and to let him have a look at the queen from time to time during her pregnancy so that she has trust in him should he be required for an emergency. Cats usually kitten at night so make sure that he is prepared well in advance. Have soap and towel ready, some sterilized scissors (boiling up in water will do) and some old boiled towelling cut up into tiny squares. Paper towelling is excellent for lining the kittens' bed after birth.

Kittens may be born head first or tail first. Neither way seems to be more common and some queens seem to present head and tail alternately as a matter of course. The queen usually likes to have

her owner present and to be stroked and soothed quietly while in labour. Most queens deal instinctively with the new-born kitten and clean the membranes from the head, licking hard to stimulate breathing. They also sever the umbilical cord and clean up the placenta, just in time to deal with the next kitten as it emerges.

Now and again the female giving birth just seems to have no idea of the right procedure for coping with her babies, and then the owner must take over and this is where the equipment comes in.

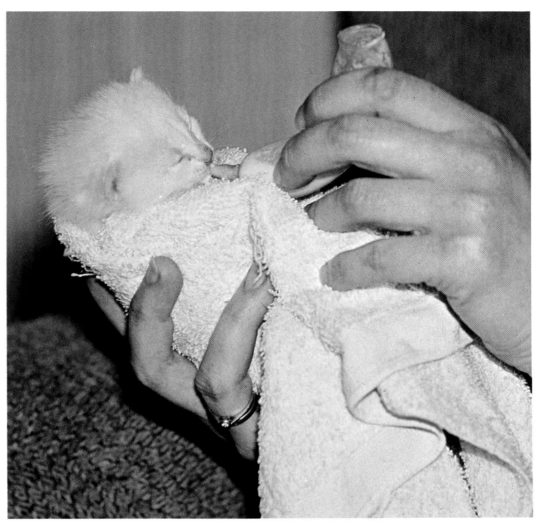

Each kitten in the litter finds its own nipple and is likely to feed at the same position right through its infancy (left). After feeding (below left), the queen washes the kittens well, and then settles down with them to rest. Orphan kittens may be handreared with a syringe, or doll's feeding bottle (right). Kittens are born blind, with tightly sealed eyelids, and the eyes gradually open, usually between three and ten days, according to the variety. These Red Abyssinians (below) are five days old and their eyes are still firmly closed.

First the hands must be well washed, rinsed and dried. The small squares of boiled towelling are used to rub the membranous material from the wet kitten, and to clear the nose and mouth. The kitten is then held head down on the palm of the left hand and rubbed from tail to head with more towelling squares until practically dry and squealing lustily. The cord can be cut with blunt, sterile scissors which will help to clamp the ends. Cut about one inch from the kitten's body and squeeze the end of the cord with a small piece of cotton wool dipped in an astringent antiseptic solution to prevent a haemorrhage. Please do not forget, this is only done in an emergency; it is always best left to the mother cat whenever possible.

An average litter for foreign cats is five kittens, whereas Longhaired and British Shorthaired cats usually have three or four kittens. When all the kittens are born, the little mother will settle down and gather them all to her to nurse. She may appreciate a bowl of warm milk mixed with egg and glucose, even if she is not normally a milk drinker. Make sure she is clean, by sliding out all the soiled newspapers and slipping a new pad covered with paper towelling under her and her litter. Check that she is warm enough and leave her to rest.

The first few weeks after birth are uneventful enough in most cases. The cords must be examined each day and any signs of inflammation must be reported to the veterinary surgeon, for they may need attention. Do not be afraid to handle the kittens. Pick them up firmly but gently and talk to the queen the whole time in a coaxing way. She should trust you enough to let you look at her babies. On the third day, Siamese and some of the other foreign breeds may start to open their eyes. Other breeds may not do this until ten days old. If there is any encrustation this can be bathed away with a saline solution, but the eyes must not be bathed open before they are ready. At this stage it is important that the kittening box is in an area of subdued light.

At about three weeks of age the kittens will start to toddle about and try to get out of the box. It is about now that the queen will be feeling a depletion of her calcium reserves, and if she does not take milk it is essential that her calcium level is kept up with tablets or injections. She should be having as much food as she wants and a plentiful supply of fresh water. The paper bedding in the kitten box should be changed daily.

At four weeks the babies may be able to get out of the box and be showing a keen interest in the mother's food. Tiny peaks of flaked fish or chicken can be shown to them and rubbed on their lips to introduce the taste and within another few days, they will start eating solids. About this time the mother will cease to clean up after the kittens and newspapers should be spread around, for there now comes a rather messy stage before the kittens realize where the toilet tray is kept. They soon learn, however, and some queens help by taking each kitten by its scruff and putting it firmly in the litter tray.

By eight weeks the kittens are almost independent of their mother and are virtually house-trained. They are eating various foods and drinking well from the water bowl. They can purr, and groom themselves. They can hiss at danger and come running when called. Two weeks later they can go to their new homes.

Hopefully, the kittens will go to new homes one or two at a time, and not all leave on the same day, for although the queen has finished nursing them, she will still miss their company. When the last kitten goes, she may cry and sound very much as though she is on heat. In fact, she will probably come on heat at this time and be ready for mating up again, but she should be allowed a few weeks to rest and to restock her calcium levels before embarking on another litter. Sooner or later, though, she will start to preen and roll and look hopefully out of the window. The deep cry of her "call" will shatter the silence of the peaceful house, and the breeding cycle is ready to start once again.

When the kittens are about three weeks of age, the queen, following ancient instincts, may decide to move the litter to a new nest site.

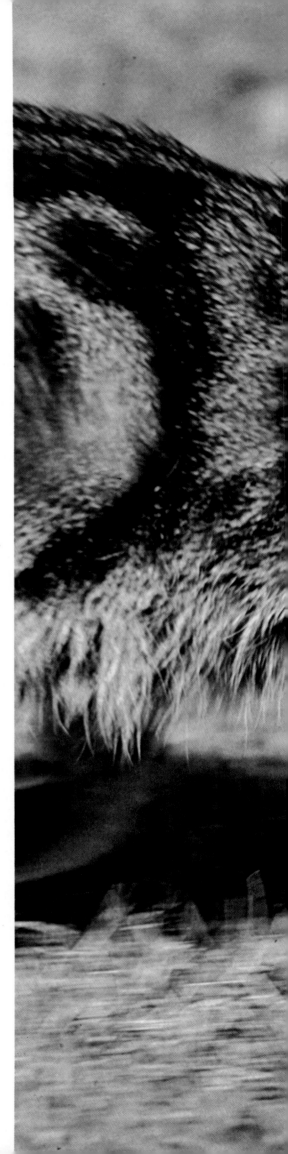

Kittens on Holiday

Each year when holiday time comes around, the problem arises as to what should be done with the family pets. Should they go along too or be left in the care of the neighbours? Or maybe they should be put into a local cattery or kennels. Some kittens take readily to long car journeys and enjoy accompanying their owners wherever they go, especially if they have been accustomed to travel from a very early age. Some kittens are more highly-strung, and it might be impracticable to take such kittens into a situation where they would prove more of a hindrance than a pleasure.

If it is your intention to take your kitten on holiday when you go, then he should be trained to car travel from the age of about 12 weeks. Take him in the car with you whenever possible, but do not let him wander around the interior unless you have someone with you to control him, preferably with a collar and lead, or a special cat harness. It is very dangerous to have a loose cat or kitten in the car while it is in motion for one never knows when there will be an emergency, and the cat could be under the clutch or brake pedal just at the critical moment.

With the help of an assistant, the kitten can be easily trained to sit in the back window of the car if he is constantly placed there and rewarded, but it is futile to expect to be able to train an older kitten to do this. The lead is essential in the car unless the kitten always travels in a carrier, for when the door is opened, he may well jump out in a strange place and become hopelessly lost. On long journeys, a deep tray with a layer of cat litter must be provided for the kitten's comfort and a bottle of water. a drinking bowl, food and a dish will take care of the rest of his needs. Even if the kitten travels happily loose in the car, it is a good idea to take a carrier along as well for emergency use, and essential if embarking on a holiday for there may be times when he must be more closely confined.

This Siamese (below) is carefully exploring an unknown area, feeling and sniffing his way. The lead makes him feel confident of returning to base. Unfortunately, one cannot adopt little kittens while holidaying abroad, and this youngster (right), basking in the Greek sunshine, must be left to fend for himself, due to the many restrictions on bringing animals into air terminals and ports.

Many hotels and motels accept cats and kittens in the rooms, and it is up to each owner to make sure that the animal does not do any damage or make a mess, otherwise the management might revoke the arrangements for future visitors. Camping and caravan or trailer sites are usually well endowed with holidaying pets. Some owners take portable runs along with them, some keep the animals on long running leads and others, bravely, turn them loose.

Many families take the family kitten for holidays afloat and cats do seem to take to life on board a boat without too much discomfort. The important thing to watch with a very young kitten is that it does not wander over the side without realizing that the water is not just a lower deck. Older kittens seem to be more sensible and soon get their sealegs.

In Britain, owners must remember that it is foolish to take their kitten along if they holiday abroad, for upon their return, the little animal will have to go into enforced quarantine for a period of six calendar months. In this case it is much better to make arrangements for the pet to be looked after by a reputable boarding cattery in the first instance.

British boarding catteries have, by law to be fully licensed by the local authority after inspection by a team of veterinary

surgeons and public health officials, who satisfy themselves that the accommodation is safe and adequate, clean and well-maintained, and that there are fire and safety precautions in operation. The proprietors must be well experienced in all aspects of cat care, and agree to abide by many regulations if the licence is granted.

The boarding licence has to be renewed each year, and the same inspection is carried out. This means that a successful boarding cattery must not only be run by cat-loving people, they must also be able to have the regular maintenance carried out, and keep all the chalets, runs and equipment in good working order.

Kittens on holiday must be watched carefully to prevent them straying. This little kitten (left) could easily become lost in the hayfield. Boarding catteries (bottom left) care for the kitten while the owner is on holiday, and high standards of expertise and hygiene are required before the local authorities grant a boarding licence. Perhaps it is best to have a very young kitten looked after by a kind neighbour or friend (below).

Having found a boarding cattery within easy reach of your home, telephone for an appointment to view, several weeks before you wish to make your booking. Do not just arrive and expect to be shown around. Cattery owners are very busy people and their charges are their main concern. It may not be convenient just at that time – the animals may be expecting their food and a visitor will get them upset and frustrated. They may have just been settled for a siesta, or for the night, and a good cattery owner will not have them disturbed. If you do turn up unexpectedly and are refused, ask for an appointment to return for a look around. You can also check on terms and feeding arrangements and probably weigh up whether or not you like the look of the proprietor, and the premises.

On being given a tour of the cattery, there are a few important things to look for. Firstly any cats that are boarding should be sitting around in the runs, sunning themselves if it is a pleasant day. There should be no heavy cat odour, and no mess in the runs. The runs should be preferably of concrete and very safely wired in. Each door should lead into some form of safety area so that a nervous cat, bolting past the assistant, cannot get right away. The runs should be roomy enough for the assistant to get into for

cleaning purposes, and long enough to provide an adequate exercise area for the cats. It is essential that cats cannot touch noses between runs as this is how any infection will be spread through the cattery. The runs should have a gap of at least three feet between them or be terraced, with solid partitioning of fibre glass or wire-reinforced plastic sheet between each one.

Each cat should have its own accommodation, or at least share only with other cats or kittens from the same home. The cat houses can be of any construction, but timber is the warmest. They must be large enough to house the cat comfortably with its bed, toilet bowl, food and water so that on rainy days, the cat still has room enough to stretch and exercise without going into the run. The compartments should be painted and have some form of washable floor covering, and the whole should look neat, workmanlike and clean.

Ask about feeding and whether or not your kitten can have his own special diet. See if he may bring his own bedding and toys along with him, and be sure that the cattery only takes fully vaccinated cats.

You may wish to inspect several catteries in your area before you decide, but do not be swayed by the prices quoted. The cheapest cattery may not prove to be the

best bargain if you return from holiday and find you are faced with a huge veterinary bill. Good catteries cost-in the price of yearly repairs, painting and replacement of wire and equipment. They feed good varied diets to owners' requirements and ensure that the cattery is staffed day and night. This has to be paid for by the owners of their charges and you may be sure that a cut-price cattery cuts down on more than its profits.

When you have decided on the most suitable cattery for your kitten, make a firm booking and pay the deposit if required. Make sure that your kitten has had any necessary injections well in advance, and on the allotted day, take him along safely in his carrier. Please do not be affronted if the cattery owner looks him over very thoroughly for signs of ill-health, parasites or diarrhoea. It is in

the interests of all concerned that you both know the condition of your kitten on his arrival, for you will hope to pick him up in good condition upon your return.

Leave him in the capable hands complete with diet sheet, bedding and toys, and do not linger over your goodbyes. He may fret for a day or so, but if he has been sensibly reared and handled, there is no reason whatever why he should not enjoy his holiday as much as you will enjoy yours.

Fees for boarding are usually paid in advance, and you should collect your kitten on the day agreed, for the kitten's accommodation may well be booked for another boarder that evening. If you cannot get back as arranged, then it is only common courtesy to telephone or send a telegram of explanation. There may be a form of indemnity for you to sign also.

This is to protect the cattery owner should there be an accident or an outbreak of illness in the cattery while your kitten is in residence. The cattery cannot take in boarders if there are sick cats on the premises, and the owner will take every precaution to ensure that no sickening cats are admitted, hence the thorough inspection of your own pet. However, some cats may be "carriers" of disease, and while looking perfectly healthy themselves can infect others on the same premises. If your cat does get sick while boarding you may be sure that the very experienced proprietor will do everything for his comfort and well-being and the veterinary surgeon will be called without delay.

A good outdoor cattery, with an adequate air flow and kept in good, hygienic conditions, will not present an

undue risk for your healthy kitten, but if possible, try to avoid boarding him at the peak holiday period which is from the beginning of August until about the second week in September, or at Bank or Public holidays. If you can take an early holiday, so much the better. There will be fewer inmates in the cattery and therefore less risk of infection.

While loose in strange surroundings, kittens may climb trees (left) or otherwise get into dangerous situations. They may be tempted by streams or fishponds (below) and therefore should be supervised until they have realized possible sources of danger for themselves. The kitten should be taken into its boarding run in a carrying basket or box (right) and allowed to explore the new area at leisure.

Upon your return, you may be surprised when your kitten, instead of rushing to greet you, prefers to curl around and rub against the legs of the cattery owner. Kittens have very short memories and two weeks can have a great effect on loyalties. Do not be too upset, though, for he will remember you when you pick him up and start talking to him, and once he is safely back home, he will rush about the house with delight.

Travelling in buses and trains can be hazardous for the kitten, and he should always be confined to his carrier for such journeys. If the kitten is very noisy or the train is extra crowded, he may have to travel in the guard's van, and it will be necessary, in any case, to purchase a ticket for him. Cats may be sent unaccompanied by train, but it is not advisable to send them this way if a change of train is necessary, for the container may be forgotten for a while and the frightened animal be left for several hours on a crowded platform amid bustling feet.

On short flights within the British Isles, and internal flights in other countries, kittens are allowed to travel as excess baggage. They may be permitted in the cabin of the aircraft at the discretion of the aircrew but usually travel in the hold; therefore, it is essential that a wooden travelling box is acquired, or at least one which is substantial enough to withstand battering by other weighty items in the event of turbulent weather conditions. The box must be able to withstand crushing and should have a sturdy door, airholes and carrying handles. Most airlines can provide suitable containers at reasonable prices upon request.

Whether travelling or holidaying with your kitten, the essential thing to remember is that he is out of his natural environment, and may well act in an unpredictable way. He must be kept under control at all times, or he may become frightened and run off, joining the ever-increasing number of strays. It can be very difficult to recapture a kitten that has run away outside his home territory and many futile hours may be spent unless a little care and thought is exercised. Unlike a dog, a kitten will not come when called if he is very scared, and can cover a lot of ground in a very short space of time. Weigh up the problems of boarding against the problems of taking him along. The boarding cattery probably comes out with the least.

While exploring, the kitten may come face to face with the unexpected, as in this encounter (above), or he may find a vantage point and hide, weighing up the surrounding area before taking steps.

Kitten Behaviour

The character and behaviour of any kitten is determined in part by its genetic make-up, that is the inborn traits that it has inherited from its parents, plus conditioned responses that it has acquired since birth. The brain of the newborn kitten has many undeveloped areas, and the tiny creature goes through a sensitive period in which information vital to its survival is processed and stored. Most creatures have this type of brain development when young, and the sensitive period varies as regards duration and timing from species to species.

In the kitten, which is born blind, rather deaf and very fragile, its inborn instincts at birth enable it to crawl towards the warmth of its mother, to seek a nipple, to suckle, and to scrabble with its forepaws against its littermates, should they get between it and the food supply. Kittens picked up at birth show no reaction to the handling, but within 24 hours, on being picked up, will hiss and tense the muscles of the spine. Many breeders leave their kittens completely alone with the mother, in a darkened box or cupboard, for the first three weeks of their lives, while others handle them daily, and it is interesting to know that those handled a great deal appear to grow up with more intelligence and with better temperament than those which are left severely alone.

The brain has many connections and junctions between the thousands of fibres which carry the constant messages being processed and these junctions form in the first few weeks of life. It seems that the slight stress caused to the well-handled kittens causes more junctions to form, and this, in turn, gives a better-developed brain than in the unstressed kitten. It has also been noticed that older kittens given plenty of toys and companionship also grow into more intelligent and even-tempered adults than those left alone for hours with little to amuse them.

A knowledge of the sensitive periods in the early weeks of the kitten's life, then, can help the owner to do several things to ensure that the adult cat will be the sort of cat he really wants. Obviously, enriching the kitten's life could be taken too far, and the traits which are amusing in a tiny kitten, such as leaping to its owner's shoulder from the rear at every opportunity, are not so funny when performed by a 12 pound adult, especially when the trick is performed as a surprise!

For the breeder, the best advice would seem to be to handle the new litter each day for a moment or two, just gently lifting each kitten, perhaps taking the opportunity to examine for any signs of weakness or defect. As the days pass and the kittens open their eyes, they will continue to hiss. Then, as focussing improves, they will begin to look at the breeder, the ears will twitch as the hearing develops and gradually they will get to accept and even enjoy the contact.

Long before the kittens eat solids, they will, if they have been handled a great deal, mew at the sound of the breeder's voice and try to toddle out of the maternity box. Kittens unused to human contact will push behind the mother, trying to escape from notice. An extreme is seen in farm litters, where the mother may be quite tame, but the kittens, having been hidden from view from birth, are rarely seen, difficult to catch, and likely to be wild and impossible to handle safely without weeks of careful coaxing.

Apart from the extra brain development in handled kittens, learning plays a part in the growth of an even temperament. Animals learn by experience, and each time a kitten is handled and returned to its mother it learns that no harm has come to it, so will be less afraid next time. The unhandled kitten has not learned this fact during the brief sensitive period, so it will find the learning process more difficult.

Sensitive periods are brief, and in the kitten, the brain is almost mature at five weeks. All the senses function by this time, but the motor development, that is the co-ordination of muscles, takes a little longer. The first week, as we have said, is spent in nursing and sleeping, but if carefully watched, the kittens, curled close to the mother cat, will twitch and quiver constantly as if dreaming. They are experiencing the sleep that we humans have during part of each night, known as Rapid Eye-Movement Sleep, or REM. During this sleep we all dream, and, it is thought, sift the experiences of the day, committing important parts to our long-term memory. Perhaps the tiny kitten is also sifting and storing the few experiences that it has had and is building the beginnings of its memory.

Smell is well developed in the newborn kitten, and this sense guides it to the warmth and security of the mother's nipple. If lifted and placed outside the nest, the kitten will show distress; its head will bob on the weak neck and turn feebly from side to side, and it will mew plaintively, trying to pick up the mother's scent, crawling around in circles. Any mother cat worth her keep will not stand for this treatment and will scoop up the kitten by the neck and take it back to the nest without delay.

Kittens, especially the Foreign varieties like the Siamese (above) use their paws as well as their eyes and noses to explore and test new objects. They will also pat at new companions, half in fear and half in anger.

As the kitten grows older, it will make little excursions from the nest and seems to be able to follow its own odour trail back again. In the early days, kittens cannot raise themselves up on their legs, and this may help in spreading the odour trail, as the whole body is dragged along the ground. The body is raised up onto the legs at about two to three weeks of age and it is at this point that play behaviour can be first observed. At three and a half weeks, the kittens will pat each other, perform washing movements, will roll over and play. They will, however, still require the stimulation of the mother's tongue for emptying bladder and bowels.

By four weeks, kittens start to show an interest in the mother's food bowl and may attempt to eat solid food. When they do, the mother will stop cleaning up their tail-ends and they will begin to use one corner of the nest for toilet purposes. Some mother cats resent this anti-social behaviour and will carry the kittens to her own toilet tray. An experienced breeder provides a shallow tray with soft, torn tissue at this time, just outside the nest box, and the kittens soon learn to use it.

At this age, the littermates start to play quite rough games with one another, and begin jumping on and biting the mother cat's tail, which she swishes from side to side encouragingly. This play behaviour is training for the hunting of prey which the cat would need in the wild, for survival. The better the co-ordination learned during kitten-play, the more successful the adult hunter.

It is fascinating to watch young kittens at play. The average litter size is five for most breeds, and kittens usually pair off for play purposes, often leaving the smallest of the litter to play with the mother cat. If she is not available, the odd kitten will join in with one of the other pairs, and there will be biting, clawing, squirming bundles of kitten all over the floor. These violent skirmishes produce no scars or bruises, and last for about 10 minutes at a time, after which the kittens return to the nestbox for a sleep or a feed. Problems arise when, through unfortunate circumstances, or perhaps a poor breeding queen, only one kitten is born or survives, and this needs very special care at this formative age. The play provided by the other kittens in a normal litter must be compensated for by extra attention by the breeder, who must play with the kitten simulating normal kitten play as nearly as possible, rolling it over and gently shaking, pushing along the floor and perhaps teasing with a small, soft toy.

Lone kittens can grow up to be most neurotic and difficult cats, quite probably because they are not given enough practise in being kittens at the sensitive time. Kittens reared by hand in solitary conditions have no means of knowing, in fact, that they are cats at all, and many problems have been encountered through lack of forethought by the kind persons who have taken so much care in providing all the physical needs. One such case has been recorded, in which a mother cat died in giving birth to her litter, and only one tiny baby survived. This little female was lovingly bottle-reared and kept in an otherwise cat-less household until she matured. She was an excellent example of her breed, and because of her unfortunate start in life was kept confined to the house, and not exposed to any danger of infection by being shown. She came into season at 10 months, and then again three weeks later, when it was decided to mate her to a local, prize studcat. The little queen was terrified of the advances made by the gentle male and although many attempts were made over the next two years, she would never mate, and was eventually spayed.

Mother cats allowed their freedom often bring home prey for their kittens, and spend much time batting it to and fro and encouraging the kittens to pounce and bite. The kittens soon learn to jump right onto the dead mouse and bite at the neck

while grasping the animal with their sharp claws. The neck-biting action seems to be inborn, and having firmly grasped the prey in this manner, the kitten will be seen to glance wide-eyed from side to side, emitting warning growls to keep his brothers and sisters away from his prize.

The six-week-old kitten has a highly developed play technique and in this uses all the motor actions that he will require in adult life, for hunting, travelling over rough terrain, and mating. All these actions can be observed during kitten play, as can the techniques used for fighting and defense. At the start of a game, kittens will chase each other, taking turns, the one fleeing, turning from side to side, using its tail as a rudder to execute sharp manoeuvres. The one chasing runs with head up and tail erect and often fluffed out. When they collide, the roles are reversed. If one kitten is "cornered" it will stand up in a defensive posture, often with paws raised, like a miniature prize-fighter, and, if attacked will use both teeth and claws for defense.

In order to look as fierce and as large as possible, the kitten that is on the defensive will turn sideways on to its attacker. The hair on the body and all along the tail will stand up and the kitten will raise itself up on tiptoes. If the attacker, undaunted by such a show of strength, continues to advance, the defensive kitten will flatten the ears back on the head and crouch down, still sideways on, and emit warning growls. Should the attacker continue to approach further, the defensive kitten will shriek and roll over, defending itself with all four paws and teeth. Kittens very rarely play as roughly as this, but it is all good practice for adult life.

In more gentle play, kittens perpetually crouch in wait for each other, then spring, landing upon the back of a littermate and bite at the neck, just as they would leap onto and bite prey. The attacked kitten will roll quickly over and rake at the attacker with its hindpaws, claws fully extended. Then the defensive kitten takes its turn at being the attacker. All this exercise is beneficial to the kitten in learning co-ordination and in developing the muscles used in crouching, pouncing and gripping. Very rarely, kittens may mount each other as in the mating of adults, but no other sexual actions take place.

A whole range of expressions may be seen in kittens, such as the yawn of boredom, and the concentration of the little tabby performing its toilet routine (left). Mother cats grasp their kittens firmly right around the neck in order to lift and transport them safely.

Lone kittens play somewhat differently, and seem to have periods of each day when violent self-play is a necessity. If no toys are available, the kitten will crouch down, look at an imaginary prey, swish its tail from side to side and look very excited with ears pricked. It will then spring forward and chase the imaginary prey between its paws, and might even roll over and chase its own tail. To solicit someone into playing with it, the kitten will roll on one side, then the other at its owner's feet. If the tummy is lightly rubbed, the hand will be gently grasped and nipped, or raked with the hind paws. All this is inviting play.

When playing with the lone kitten, the toys provided must be imaginative and fulfil the kitten's needs. A rabbit's paw is ideal for tossing to and fro, batting along the smooth kitchen floor, for pouncing on and for imaginary killing. A ball of crinkly paper makes enticing noises as it tries to unroll itself. Spiders made from twisted pipecleaners act in a most realistic way; when one leg is grasped by the kitten's mouth, the other legs twist around and cause great excitement. The owner, playing with the kitten, must think like another cat and behave accordingly. Toys must be jerked convincingly or thrown carefully, and above all the kitten must never be made to feel foolish, or laughed at, for this it will find unforgivable.

Most kittens are naturally very clean in their habits, and it is an inborn trait of the cat family to bury all traces of its excreta. A kitten kept in the home, therefore, must be provided with a toilet tray in which it can dig a hole, then be able to cover up. Proprietary brands of cat litter are available, and have deodorizing properties, but some cats find these distasteful. Your kitten may prefer to use sawdust, sand, earth, peat or even torn toilet tissue. One thing is for sure, though, if the litter is wet or soiled the kitten will use the dining room carpet, and once that habit is formed it proves very hard to break. Bad habits can be broken in kittens by scolding for wrong-doing and praising for doing well, but in the case of toilet training, smell is the prime sense, and the kitten will think it is all right to use a spot that he can smell has been used before. Most household cleansers fail to remove completely kittens' smells, and this should be borne in mind during preliminary housetraining.

Feeding habits must be formed early in kittenhood, for in the wild, animals learn what is safe to eat by trial and error. Cats will not usually eat tainted foods, but it is very important that the kitten, at weaning, is given a very varied diet for if given only one type of food, may well become "hooked" on this for life. Such a diet would not build him to a strong healthy adult, and could cause problems of deficiency in some vitamins or minerals. Small feeds of quite different foods should be offered each day, and any new food can be mixed with an old favourite until it is readily acceptable.

The kitten washes itself thoroughly from about 12 weeks of age onwards, and follows a set routine for this procedure. Usually after meals, he will sit down and meticulously wash a paw. When this is quite damp and clean, he will use it to wash over his face and ear, then repeat the process with the opposite paw. Each side of the body then gets a thorough grooming with the rough tongue, then each back leg, finally the tail, after which the kitten feels quite tidy and relaxed and settles down for a long nap. This behaviour often becomes social, and kittens or cats living together will often groom each other in the same manner.

Kittens love being stroked and petted, and will often push their heads right into the hand of the owner to ask for this type of contact. Sometimes the act of stroking and fondling a young kitten will cause it to start nursing on an arm or sleeve, and it may also start kneading with the paws as in the act of nursing from its mother. This should not be encouraged in the kitten, although it must not be deprived of affection, for some kittens, perhaps weaned too early, start bad habits, such as wool-sucking, and the ingested lumps of wool cause internal problems. If a kitten gets carried away in this manner, stop the stroking and start up a good, active game instead.

With most pleasurable activities, a kitten will perform a phenomenon known as purring. It will start to purr when tiny and nursing from its mother, and will purr for its owner from about the age of six weeks when stroked about the head and chin, or down the spine. Some kittens purr so much that they drool at the same time. Purring can be soft or loud, and some sick or injured cats, when in pain, still purr, but with a harsher note. Some purrs are on a monotone, especially in young kittens, while older cats can have two-tone or three-tone purrs. Whatever the sound, there is nothing quite so relaxing after a hard day's work, than to sit quietly with a soft kitten upon ones knees and to let oneself breathe quietly in rhythm with the contented purring.

A kitten brought up in an enriched environment, with lots of toys, will grow up into an intelligent adult cat.
Great care must be exercised in introducing a new kitten to an older cat, who may be jealous and resentful (right).

Growling can be as varied as purring. There is the growl of alarm at an unusual sound or the very special growl performed with a mouthful of chicken or some other delicacy, when a littermate approaches. The growl accompanied by flattened ears and a swishing, fluffed up tail means danger; and there is the rather squealing growl of fear. Any kitten that is growling should be examined if the cause is not readily apparent for it may follow an unseen injury and could point to a fractured leg or paw, or even a fracture of the hard palate caused by jumping down from a height and striking the chin on landing. A kitten growling and running backwards shaking its head, has almost certainly suffered an injury and should be taken to the veterinary surgery, without delay.

Kittens use their voices for communication as well as for purring and growling. The mother cat has a repertoire of sounds that she makes to tell her kittens to come to her, that there is danger, that she has food and so on, and the kittens have several sounds that they make back to her in response. The pet kitten will have a mew of welcome which is quite different to the demanding one that he will give out when he is hungry. He will have another sound when searching for a favourite toy, or when he is shut out of the room and wants to get in, and when approaching maturity, if not altered, the female's "call" is quite unmistakable in its demanding tone and carrying power. Those who live with and study cats could write chapters on the voice of the cat. No animal on earth has such a range of expressions with such limited vocal chords.

As we have seen, much of the behaviour of the adult cat depends on the treatment meted out to him during his early, formative weeks, but even temperamental or neurotic cats can have their natures improved by careful, gentle handling. Surely it is better, though, to spend a little time and patience at the beginning to shape a kitten, feeding the mind as well as filling the stomach with nourishing foods. A few minutes' care, love and playtime each day, and life in a happy, enriched household will ensure that your kitten grows into a happy, well-balanced and pleasing pet cat.

Plenty of playthings keeps a kitten in good physical condition, lively, and alert.

The Kitten in Danger

The feline race are notorious for their acute powers of hearing, smell and sight, and for their surefootedness and the ability always to land on their feet when falling. Added to this is that they are supposed to have nine lives. So it would seem that there is little need for this chapter. However, to the tiny kitten, the strange new world into which he has been brought holds plenty of peril.

Of all the dangers facing cats today, that of a road accident must be given priority, for cats seem to have very little road sense and the veterinary hospitals are constantly busy treating road accident casualties. Many people now keep their cats in the house at all times, providing pots of grass and toilet facilities, and starting the cat off in this environment when a tiny kitten, so that it has no knowledge of the outside world, and no wish to wander abroad. Neither should the kitten be allowed to play outside under any parked cars, for he may seek the warmth and not be noticed when the owner drives away, with disastrous results.

Other dangers await the wandering kitten besides fast-moving traffic. There are large, fierce dogs which have been encouraged by thoughtless owners to chase cats, and there are strange young people who take delight in ill-treating animals. By and large, then, it would seem that the kitten is much safer kept shut up in the house. But is he?

Just as with humans, the kitten has a fair chance of meeting dangers in the home, and most of those are in the kitchen. One of the most common accidents which may befall young kittens is scalding with hot water or fat. Kittens will rub around their owner's legs while she is cooking, and spills from saucepan lids and spluttering fat can cause very nasty burns. Luckily the splashes are usually of small spots and

the thick fur protects the skin to a certain extent, but it is a good plan to shut young kittens away in another room while cooking, especially deep-frying, is going on.

Veterinary surgeons have many cases brought to them, usually too late I fear, of kittens which have been inadvertently shut in the refrigerator, the washing machine, or the tumble-dryer. Kittens sneak into the refrigerator after all sorts of titbits, so it is important to check before closing the door. The warmth of the open tumble-drier may encourage a small kitten to crawl inside, so again, the interior should be checked before switching on. The lid should always be tightly closed while the washing machine is working, for although most kittens are scared away by the noise, there are some whose curiosity overcomes the fear and they cannot resist playing with the swishing suds, sometimes with fatal results.

It seems that most young kittens are kept in the kitchen of their new home at first, and this is where they may be at most risk during normal housekeeping activities. Obviously, one wants the new pet near at hand whenever possible, but it would be a better plan to shut him safely in another room while anything hazardous is going on, at least until he grows a little larger and easier to keep in sight.

Fear has caused this kitten to flatten its body and ears into a typical submissive pose, ready for a fight but poised for flight.

It is very easy to tread on tiny kittens for they are always at one's heels and many have been injured by having someone step back onto a leg or tail. They are also apt to follow through closing doors and it is easy to slam a door onto the kitten's head or body. Because of the dangers, most breeders with a whole litter toddling around make use of special kitten play-pens, to keep the tiny creatures confined while much activity is going on. Then when all is quiet, they are let out to romp and explore.

During the period when they are cutting new teeth, small kittens bite and gnaw on anything. It is important not to have any live electric cord leading to lamps or equipment, that the kitten may bite through. His tiny teeth are razor sharp and can easily penetrate the plastic casing, making a connection and causing electro-cution. Chewing on string is dangerous too for the end may be swallowed, and more and more of the length taken down the gullet. This is then impossible to draw out and dangerous to allow to pass through, so veterinary treatment is re-quired. Kittens have been known to play with thread attached to a needle, and in the same way, swallow the thread, pulling the needle into the soft area at the back of the throat. Again veterinary treatment is urgently required.

Kittens rarely ingest poisonous sub-stances as most toxic products are dis-tasteful to them; however, there is one thing that they cannot resist although licking it may cause rapid collapse and death. That is the anti-freeze product for putting in car radiators in the winter. For some reason the smell is very attractive to most cats, so it is important to make sure that your kitten is out of the garage when the radiators are prepared for the cold weather.

Phenol-based disinfectants can be lethal to all cats and the small kitten is par-ticularly susceptible. The danger is in using the product without carefully measuring the correct dilution, or in leaving pools of dampness on the newly washed kitchen floor. The floor may be germ-free, but when the kitten paddles through the damp patches the phenol constituents are absorbed through his pads into his bloodstream and give rise to very unpleasant symptoms. For the same reason food and water bowls should be thoroughly rinsed clear of detergent before re-use.

Dangers in the home are many and varied for the young kitten: the hot stove may burn his delicate paws, and electric cables could cause a bad shock. Kittens often climb onto warm car tyres and may be injured if undetected.

Creosote and paint tins are often explored by the young kitten and the stuff gets onto the coat. The kitten must be prevented from licking the areas and must be carefully examined to see that no paint is actually on the skin. The paint-covered hair must be clipped away without delay, and any areas of skin cleaned as well as possible using lard or margarine. The veterinary surgeon must be contacted for advice. Make sure the kitten is shut well away from any part of the house where decorating is going on for this is a case where prevention is much, much easier than the cure.

Some of the vaporizing fly-killing products are harmful to young kittens, although only if too great a concentration of vapour fills the room. Most packs give the cubic footage recommended for each vapour strip or container, and this should be carefully read if there is to be a kitten loose in the room. More worrying is the fact that these vaporizing products cause the insects to become disorientated at first, when they buzz in small circles on the floor, and this is when they become an attractive game for the kitten to bat around and possibly eat. Most kittens will only eat the first fly, which they find so distasteful that they immediately regurgitate it. Others, though, may eat many such flies and become quite ill, needing veterinary treatment.

Aerosol sprays for air-freshening and for disinfection must be used cautiously, having shut the kitten well out of the way before use, and aerosol sprays containing pest powder or liquid must never be used in the kitten's coat. Most of these products contain ingredients which are extremely toxic to cats in general and to small kittens in particular. Products made for use on dogs are generally quite unsuitable for cats in any case, for some substances which are completely safe for dog care will prove fatal if used on a kitten or cat.

Kittens find most insects quite fascinating to play with and to chase, and in most cases it does no harm, the insect merely flies away. In late summer, however, there is a danger from wasps which become fairly torpid and are inclined to get in the house and crawl around the floor unnoticed. The kitten may catch and swallow such a wasp and in most cases will be stung inside the throat or at the back of the mouth. This serious situation must receive the veterinary surgeon's skilled treatment without fail, for the stung area may swell very quickly and can cause asphyxiation.

Some houseplants are poisonous to cats and should not be cultivated where there is a small kitten in the house, for although most cats chew on houseplants occasionally, if there is no grass available, they usually avoid those which are toxic to them. Kittens, however, perpetually teething, will chew on anything most of the time, and a trailing houseplant can be very tempting. The plants of the Philodendron family are those which, if ingested, may cause severe vomiting and should be kept away from the kitten. Although upsetting, it is not thought that any houseplant is fatally toxic to cats.

Even in the garden, care must be taken with insecticides and weedkillers. A lawn, freshly treated and before it has rained, should be taboo for the kitten, for it is certain that the substance will be absorbed through the pads of his feet and enter the bloodstream. Slug-bait is another lethal factor as far as the feline race is concerned as well as killing slugs most effectively. Both the bait and the poisoned slug will, if ingested, kill a kitten very rapidly, and there is no known antidote.

Most substances used for baiting rats and mice also prove fatal to cats, although in some cases antidotes are known. Cats and kittens rarely take the poisoned bait but may catch and eat the poisoned rodents with tragic results. This is another instance where it seems that pets are much safer if confined to the house. Even non-toxic rats and mice can be hazardous if caught by the kitten, for most are infested with parasites, both externally and internally, some of which may be transmitted to the young cat.

Being great climbers, kittens often venture too far up a favourite tree, or out onto a dangerous windowledge, and the worst thing to do in such instances is to panic, for this is when the kitten will become frightened and may fall. If left alone,

chances are that he will find his own way back to safety. If he is really scared, he may loosen his grip and slip. Kittens are not afraid of heights and are quite adept at extricating themselves from difficult situations. Sometimes, though, the tree is really too high and it is necessary to get an extending ladder to reach well past the kitten. Someone with a head for heights should go to the rescue, armed with a zipped-top bag into which the kitten can be safely dropped and secured before the descent.

It has been known for a kitten to sail through an open bedroom window when in hot pursuit of an insect, suffering dreadful injuries, so the moral here is to keep the kitten out of the bedroom. Kittens are so boisterous in their play that all danger is forgotten, and they have also been known to run straight into unguarded open fires, and to run up and knock over oil heaters, causing outbreaks of fire.

Finally, the kitten may be in danger from the cat thieves, gangs of unscrupulous men who visit different areas, usually at night, and coax any wandering cat or kitten into their nets. These unfortunate animals are then sold for research purposes or for their pelts, and although this trade is obviously illegal, it still goes on. The golden rule is obviously to make sure that your cats are in at night for few thieves would risk cat-snatching in the daytime.

This chapter has indicated some of the hazards that may face a young and inexperienced kitten, and also a more mature cat, and is designed to underline the simple precautions and the common-sense attitude necessary before taking the young creature into the home as a pet. With a little forethought, your kitten will sail through his formative months and give you years of pleasure as an adult cat, never in danger of losing even the first of his nine lives.

While decorating the home, the kitten should be shut safely in another part of the house, for paint, and the substances for cleaning it off, may prove fatal to him (left).
Young kittens often climb onto dangerous objects (above right) and must be carefully lifted down so that they do not fall and, perhaps, fracture a limb. They also chew on unsuitable objects, like this bamboo shoot (right), which could damage the delicate lining of the mouth and tongue.
The lost kitten (overleaf) will wail pitifully, hoping to be rescued by its mother or its new owner, and will usually stay in one spot until help is at hand.

The Kitten's Health

The best time to have your first meeting with the veterinary surgeon is while your kitten is in perfect health, that is, if he has not been vaccinated against Feline Infectious Enteritis, or Panleucopaenia, then he should be taken along for his injection. The appointment must be made, perhaps by telephone, and the kitten transported safely in his carrier, to the surgery. Before administering the vaccine by injection, the veterinary surgeon will carefully and thoroughly examine your pet. Vaccine can only be given to a perfectly healthy kitten. Depending upon the make and type of vaccine used, either one dose, or two separate doses with a 14 day interval between, may be given and the kitten should not be allowed to contact other cats until immunity is complete.

The veterinary surgeon will tell you whether or not he considers a worming course is necessary for your kitten, and will also discuss a suitable age for neutering if you have decided against breeding. He will check that the teeth are all coming through well and that there is no infection of the gums. He will, if requested, check the ears and show you how to clip back the claws. Establish a happy relationship at this time with the veterinary surgeon for you may need him some day in an emergency.

While a kitten is eating normally, and passing normal faeces without any distress, while his eyes look bright and he is playful and alert, then there is likely to be very little wrong with his health. The first signs of illness in the kitten are loss of appetite, listlessness and an open appearance of the coat. This is caused by the hairs being held erect for the kitten is running a temperature. The third eyelids or "haws" may also be just visible in the corners of the eyes.

These symptoms may be caused by teething troubles and a quick look in the mouth may confirm this to be the case. Kitten's second teeth often erupt before the milk teeth are ready to be shed and the two sets make the mouth sore and uncomfortable. The condition may soon right itself and soft food can be given until the soreness wears off. Otherwise the offending teeth must be professionally removed. The same symptoms could point to the onset of one of the infectious diseases also, especially if the kitten has been playing with others, or has recently been staying in a boarding cattery.

Feline illness can be divided into two main groups. The first embraces those diseases which arise from outside causes. These are infectious and contagious diseases caused by viruses, bacteria and parasites. Although few in number, they are usually serious, and may be fatal in the young kitten. The second group covers illness arising from internal malfunction and are mainly upsets of the digestive tract, many of which are caused by faulty diet.

Possibly the most common of the infectious diseases in the cat is the one commonly known as Cat "Flu", of which there are many different strains. Two main viruses can give rise to this potentially fatal illness, and secondary infection of streptococci and staphylococci makes matters worse. The kitten which contracts Cat "Flu" is depressed and loses condition rapidly, having stopped eating because his throat is sore. In some types of "Flu" he may drool great rivulets of saliva from between his closed lips, and may sneeze and cough from time to time. As the days pass his eyes will water, then the discharge gradually thickens and may cause the eyes and nostrils to close completely. In other types of "Flu", the mouth becomes

very ulcerated but there is no eye or nasal discharge.

Cat "Flu" is contracted by the kitten by inhaling droplets containing the infectious micro-organisms sneezed from an infected cat, or from feeding from infected bowls. There is nothing that can combat the virus, but a course of antibiotics to check the secondary bacterial infections and the careful nursing care described later are the most valuable aids to recovery.

Feline Infectious Enteritis, or F.I.E., is an acute and often fatal disease which mainly affects cats under one year of age. This is why the early vaccination previously mentioned is so important. The disease may be very rapid in its progress, and breeders of pedigree kittens have known a litter to be playing normally in the morning and all quite dead by the evening of the same day. The kitten first starts a very high fever, the appetite is lost and he is depressed and may vomit. The temperature then drops very low and the kitten dehydrates rapidly, maybe sitting hunched over his water bowl but not drinking. A comatose state then follows, followed rapidly by death. Although the disease is called Feline Infectious Enteritis, there is no diarrhoea in the early stages; this only occurs if the kitten survives through the first two or three days.

Recently isolated during research were the viruses responsible for two deadly feline diseases, Feline Infectious Anaemia, or F.I.A., and Feline Infectious Peritonitis, or F.I.P. Treatment has been successful in the first, but for F.I.P. death is inevitable. The onset of both diseases is similar; the kitten looks lethargic and depressed. In F.I.A. a high fever develops and the temperature may reach a staggering 107°F. The eyelids, tongue and

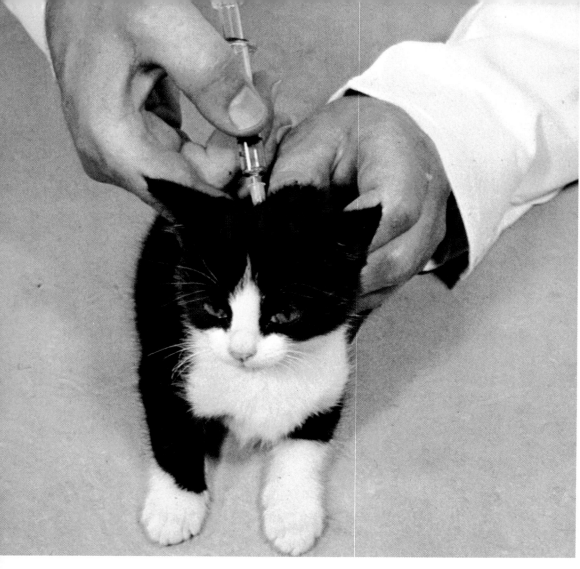
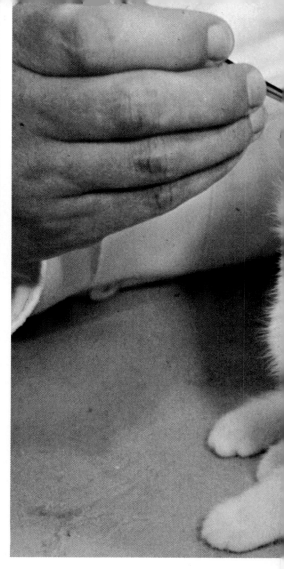

mucous membranes gradually become pale and as the disease progresses, there will be difficulty in breathing and terminal vomiting. Blood transfusions have been given to cats suffering from F.I.A. followed by a course of antibiotic treatment and this has proved a satisfactory cure in some cases. F.I.A. is contracted through flea infestation, the parasites carrying the infection from a sick cat to a healthy one, or may be passed from a mother to her unborn kitten.

F.I.P. follows a slow and lingering course. The early depression continues and the abdomen swells, the temperature fluctuates to very high levels, and drops below normal and the kitten gradually becomes very emaciated. Microscopic examination of body fluids is the only way in which a definite diagnosis can be made of this dread disease, and if positive, it is usually kinder to have the kitten put to sleep than allowed to live through the terminal stages.

Another disease of viral origin which has caused great concern among cat breeders all over the world is Feline Leukaemia, or FeLV. This illness is very similar to F.I.P., and the virus is spread by contact with an infected animal's saliva, urine or blood. Vaccine is available for the immunization of kittens which may become contacts of infected cats, or moving into a home where a cat with F.I.P. has been living.

Luckily, the percentage of kittens which become infected with these diseases is remarkably low, and it is the problems with general health that we will discuss now, in an A-Z of common ailments.

Abcesses are caused most frequently by the skin healing too rapidly after a deep bite or cut which has introduced bacteria well under the skin layers. The most common sites for cat-bite abcesses are on the head, paws or at the base of the tail. The first sign of trouble is that the kitten becomes listless with a raised temperature, and after careful examination, the lump will be found. Antibiotics may disperse the swelling, but much relief can be given by hot fomentations. Wring out a sponge in hand-hot water and apply it to the affected area until it cools. Repeat several times. This procedure should be carried out as often as possible–four or five times daily–until the abcess comes to a head and bursts. Then it can be cleaned with a mild antiseptic solution. If the foot is affected, it can be immersed in a jamjar of comfortably hot water and more hot water added as the jar cools. The kitten will sit comfortably on your knee on a folded towel and enjoy the relief afforded in this way. Once the abcess has burst, the open area should be kept open and antibiotic powder provided by the veterinary surgeon applied frequently after bathing. Should it close up again too soon, more pus will form under the skin. It is essential to treat an abcess quickly for if neglected, a chronic septic condition may set in which is difficult to treat effectively.

Allergies are common in kittens and may be caused by various things. Some cats are allergic to flea-bites and a condition known as flea eczema arises in which small scabs are formed in clusters on the skin and the hair breaks away, leaving patchy areas.

Some plants cause an allergic reaction if sniffed by cats, and the allergy takes the form of conjunctivitis or a condition resembling asthma.

Some kittens, especially those with Siamese in their ancestry, are allergic to milk and all milk products. The allergy may manifest itself in a skin condition similar to eczema, or in severe gastric upset, or both. Fish, if fed to excess, causes a condition known as miliary, or "fish" eczema. The skin on the spine becomes very dry and itchy, and the cat licks and scratches at the area until much of the hair is removed. Eggs can cause similar reactions to those of fish or milk

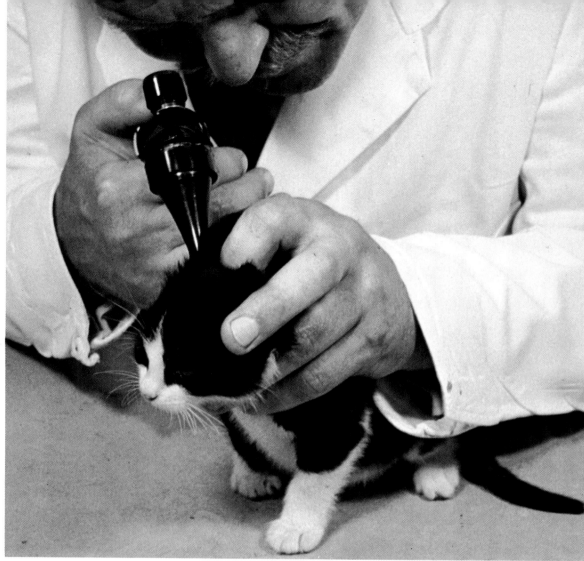

in some kittens, and in any case of skin troubles or gastric upset, the previous few days' diets should be remembered to see if there is any clue available for the condition which has arisen.

Certain drugs cause allergic reactions, and if, after veterinary treatment, the kitten is sick, has diarrhoea, is scratching, or losing coat, take him back to the surgery for a further check-up.

Anal glands are situated under the tail, and secrete a sebaceous fluid. Very occasionally, the tiny openings in each gland can become blocked, and small abcesses may form. The kitten will drag its seat along the ground and lick the area vigorously. The glands need professionally treating and the infection discharged with antibiotics.

Anaesthetics are necessary for even quite minor operations on cats and kittens, for felines are notoriously difficult to handle when in any pain or distress and can inflict nasty wounds on the veterinary surgeon and his assistants. It is important that the kitten is starved before being anaesthetized; the stomach must be empty or the kitten could choke. Twelve hours without food prior to the operation is usual. The recovery rate varies from cat to cat and depending upon the length of time that the animal has been unconscious. The kitten must be kept quiet and warm, in a safe carrier until completely conscious, for he may stagger and hurt himself. He should not be touched either, for his reflexes may not be normal and he may resent the touch and bite. If possible, leave him safely at the surgery until he has completely come round.

Antibiotics are a family of drugs which are used extensively for the treatment of secondary bacterial infections. If such treatment is prescribed for your kitten, it is essential that the correct dosage is given and for the prescribed number of days. The level of antibiotic in the body must be maintained by small, regular doses to kill the bacteria and to prevent resistant strains being formed. This treatment must only be given under veterinary supervision, and any unused pills or ointments must be destroyed, not kept and used on future occasions.

Antiseptics suitable for use in humans could prove disastrous if used on your kitten, for most are developed from chemicals known as coal-tar derivatives which are toxic to members of the cat family. The safest antiseptic to use to clean up wounds in the kitten is hydrogen peroxide, well diluted and finally rinsed away with salt water.

Artificial respiration is difficult to administer to the kitten, but in an emergency, for example after electric shock, a kitten which appears dead may be revived. Gentle swinging by the hind legs, the kitten's head hanging downwards, may be effective. Alternatively, lay the kitten on its side and press the chest gently, then relax. This is repeated about every four seconds, and while there is a heart beat, there is hope of recovery. This can be maintained until the veterinary surgeon arrives.

Aspirin can be fatal if given to your kitten, and must never be administered in any form. Few human medicines are suitable for cats, and veterinary advice should be sought before dosing a kitten with any product.

Bones can get stuck in the mouth or throat of the kitten, and cause great distress. They can usually be removed with a pair of tweezers if clearly visible, otherwise they need skilled attention. If the kitten is pawing at its mouth or drooling, wrap him very firmly, like a mummy, in a towel and have someone hold him tightly while you quickly open the mouth with a spatula or tail-end of a wooden spoon and deftly remove the bone. Unless this can be done quickly, get the kitten to the surgery immediately.

Bronchitis may develop after a respiratory disease and is distressing to witness in the young kitten. A warm, well-ventilated room is essential for nursing, and the breathing passages must be kept open with inhalations of Friars Balsam, or Vick.

Calcium is necessary in the kitten's diet to ensure proper bone formation and healthy teeth. If the kitten does not drink milk, or cannot digest it, then bonemeal or calcium tablets must be added to the diet. Wild cats get all the calcium they need by chewing up the bones of their prey; however, it could be dangerous to feed your kitten cooked bones, which may be brittle and splinter.

Canker is the term used to describe any trouble in the ear. The condition is usually caused by earmites which live and breed right down in the ear canal and need specialist treatment for complete eradication. Proprietary brands of "canker powder" should NEVER be put into the kitten's ears as they dry out the normal, healthy moist conditions and are very unlikely to cure any ear troubles.

Claws sometimes become torn and broken and swell, causing lameness, and can be treated at home in the same way as described for an abcess of the foot. If the swelling does not subside the following day, infection will have invaded the area and professional advice must be sought.

Conjunctivitis is an inflamed condition of the membranes around the eye, and may be caused by an allergy, an irritant in the eye—dust, fumes, or a scratch from another kitten–or it may herald the onset of a respiratory infectious disease. The eye should be bathed with saline solution using fresh swabs for each application, and if not much improved the following day, a visit to the veterinary surgeon is necessary.

Constipation can be caused by sudden confinement of a usually active kitten, for example when kenneled during the holiday period, or by changing to a very dry diet. Longhaired kittens may become constipated through ingesting a lot of loose hair. Having made certain that the kitten really is constipated and not straining to empty a blocked bladder, treatment may be relatively simple. Give lots of fluids and small meals of sardines or similar oily fish, and seek veterinary advice if the kitten is no better the following day.

Dehydration is a very serious condition in the kitten, needing immediate treatment, for it is a symptom of serious diseases, and the prime cause of death in some. A dehydrated kitten will suddenly look very thin and drawn, and if the skin is pulled gently away from the neck, it remains lifted, and feels dry and leathery to the touch (normal skin rolls back into place). Waste no time in getting to the surgery.

Diarrhoea is not a disease, and is most often caused in young kittens by faulty diet. Some get the condition by taking milk, some from eggs, some from liver and so on. Only experience will show which foods bring about frequent, fluid motions. Diarrhoea can also be troublesome in a kitten suffering from a heavy worm burden, and in this case the bowel must be treated first until soothed, then the

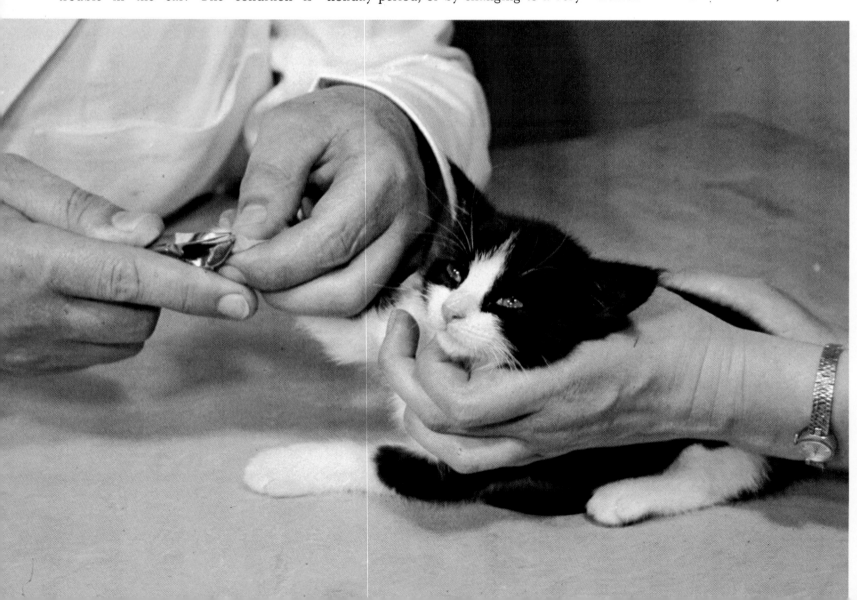

veterinary surgeon will prescribe a suitable worming medicine.

Fleas can transmit several diseases among cats, and may also be host to the tapeworm; therefore, it is important to keep your kitten free from these parasites. A very fine-toothed metal comb is the best method of checking through the coat. It is inadvisable to use insecticide sprays and powders in the coats of young kittens as they may prove to have toxic side-effects.

Fractures are sustained by kittens through being dropped, stepped on, or shut in doors. A kitten suspected of having a fracture should be lifted carefully on to a towel and placed, with the towel, in a small carrier until veterinary attention is obtained. Never try to apply splints, for you will do more harm than good and cause unnecessary pain to the kitten.

Careful trimming back of the long claws, with special clippers (left), can help prevent unwanted stropping of the furniture, and if any parasites are present in the coat, a safe insecticidal spray will be used to keep the pests at bay (right).

Gingivitis is a condition in which the gums become very inflamed and sore, and the first signs are usually when the kitten approaches its food dish eagerly, starts to eat, then gives up. An examination of the mouth will reveal a bright pink line extending along the gums. Veterinary treatment is essential because gingivitis may be the first signs of a serious illness developing in your kitten.

Haw is the name given to the nictitating membrane or third eyelid in the cat. If permanently visible in your kitten, it could mean that he is incubating a disease or has a heavy worm burden.

Injections are often used by the veterinary surgeon to ensure that the correct dose of antibiotics, or other substances, gets into the kitten's system. Vaccinations against F.I.E. are given by subcutaneous injection and are completely painless. If you are upset by the sight of a hypodermic needle, let someone else take your kitten for injections, for your distress may transmit itself to your pet.

Jaundice is a symptom of several major diseases in the cat. The eyes may change colour and the tissues take on a yellowish tinge. No time should be wasted in seeking professional advice.

Kinks are small deformities in the tail vertebrae of kittens. They cause no harm if at the extremity of the tail, but as this fault is hereditary, kittens with kinks should be neutered and not allowed to breed, for in their offspring the kink COULD be at the tail base, in which case the condition could prove rather more serious.

Licking excessively in the young kitten is a danger sign. There may be some foreign body such as a grass seed, or tick, or it may herald the onset of eczema. Try to determine the cause before rushing off to the veterinary surgery. If the licking persists and you can find no explanation, seek professional advice.

Mange is an unpleasant skin condition caused by a tiny, burrowing mite. The first signs are small, bald patches usually around the head, and the condition needs prompt attention to prevent spreading.

Nursing plays the greatest part in the kitten's recovery to health. In serious diseases, a dedicated effort must be made to pull the sick kitten through, and while the veterinary surgeon will advise and give antibiotic injections, it is the sensible nursing care of the owner that will really decide whether the kitten lives or dies.

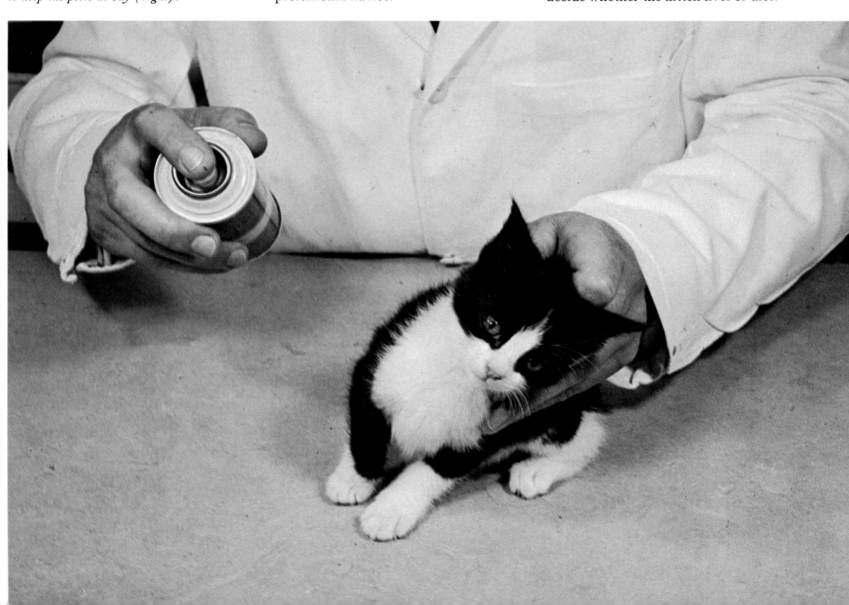

The main essentials are warmth and cleanliness. An infra-red heat lamp can be used, or constantly replenished hot water bottles, well wrapped. The eyes, nostrils and mouth must be bathed several times each day in cases of respiratory infections, and the tail end may need similar attention. The kitten should be placed on his tray and supported at regular intervals. The bedding, which should be of soft paper towelling on a thick pad of newspapers, must be changed regularly as soiled, and if the patient is collapsed, he must be turned to alternate sides several times daily and the newly exposed side gently massaged. Gentle grooming helps to keep the sick kitten alert and vaseline jelly must be applied to cracked nostrils and eyelids. If the respiratory passages are blocked, the kitten should have the jelly applied to the nose and eyelids, then

should be placed in a mesh or wicker carrier on top of a slightly smaller cardboard box holding a bowl of hot inhalant such as Friars Balsam or Vick. A plastic sheet or cloth is spread right over the whole of the carrier and box so that the inhalant permeates into the carrier and is trapped inside by the plastic covering. Five minutes is sufficient for each session which may be repeated every three or four hours. Great relief is afforded by this procedure in the most severe of respiratory illnesses.

Orphan kittens are difficult to rear by hand as they need very frequent feeding and attention day and night for the first four weeks of their lives. It is kinder to attempt to find a foster mother for orphaned kittens, as she will make a better job of rearing them than a human could.

Pot-belly in the kitten either points to infestation with worms, or to malnutrition. Proper treatment is essential after diagnosis of the cause, and will usually effect a rapid cure.

Rickets is a condition rarely seen in kittens, although some do show a range of ricket-like traits, and may be sensitive to touch around the hind-quarters. This can be counteracted by a course of calcium, by tablets or injection, and treatment should not be delayed.

Stomatitis is an inflammation of the mouth due to several causes. The kitten will stop eating and look wretched. The veterinary surgeon will examine his mouth and determine the cause. Some teeth may need attention, or the inflammation may have been caused by hot food or a sharp

bone. It may also be the first stage in the onset of a more serious infection.

Teeth are usually troublefree in kittens, although some may not shed the milk teeth when the adult set emerges, causing a sore mouth. Pieces of raw meat should be fed to young kittens from about three months onwards, for this helps the milk teeth to come out when loosened and also keeps the gums healthy.

Vomiting in kittens may be serious, especially if the substance brought up is bright yellow, or resembles beaten egg-white. Vomiting accompanied by diarrhoea and a fever is the warning that your kitten is in for something quite serious and needs immediate treatment. The regurgitation of food merely means your kitten has eaten too much, too fast.

Worms are unpleasant parasites, present in most pets. There are several types and each needs different treatment for eradication. To determine if your kitten has a worm burden, collect a sample of his motion, put it into a plastic bag and take to the veterinary surgeon, who will examine it under the microscope, identify the parasite and prescribe the correct medicine. Do not give your kitten proprietary brands of worming pills; they may do him harm.

Yeast tablets are an excellent natural tonic for kittens and some like to eat them as "sweets". One or two daily provide the kitten's requirements of Vitamin B.

Zoonoses are diseases that you may get from your kitten and these are rare. Keep your kittens free from parasites.

Do not let him sleep in your bed. Cook his food and wash his dishes separately from your own and wash your hands after touching him or his toilet tray.

Plenty of good food, healthy outdoor exercise and tender, loving care are the essentials for taking the kitten through its formative months to adulthood. Bright eyes, a clean, glossy coat and an alert, bright expression are all signs that this little black and white kitten (overleaf) is in perfect health.

Kittens on Show

Showing your kitten can be a very pleasant hobby, and cat shows are held in most civilized countries of the world. The shows are usually staged by cat clubs for their members, but are often open to non-members as well. There are several sorts of cat show. Some, held in aid of various charities, are for pet cats without pedigrees, while others are highly organized and are run under the rules of the country's governing body relating to all feline matters.

In Britain, for example, the Governing Council of the Cat Fancy elects judges and approves cat shows, which may be of Championship, Exemption or Sanction status. At Championship Shows there are Open or Breed Classes for every recognized variety of pedigree cat and kitten, and in the adult classes the winner, if of very high quality, may be awarded a coveted Champion Challenge Certificate. A cat needs three such certificates awarded by three different judges, at three shows to become a Champion in his own right. Kittens are not eligible for these certificates, but it is an honour to win a breed class, and the winners may be nominated for Best in Show awards. Each judge sends in a slip to the Show's recording table, giving the numbers of his best cat, best kitten and best neuter. These exhibits are presented to a panel of senior judges at the end of the show, and they are assessed in silence. Each judge on the panel then votes for the cat, kitten and neuter of his choice and those animals with the most votes take the awards of honour.

Other countries have slightly different procedures, and in the U.S., for example, there are several registering bodies, each with slightly different rules and regulations. In most American cat shows, there are four "rings" which count as four separate shows. The cats are judged in each ring and can win their Championship ribbons in each. In the American Cat Fanciers Association, a cat needs four Championship ribbons to complete his Championship status. If he wins in each of the four rings on one day he is thus declared a Champion.

Plenty of play activity ensures that this healthy litter of Blue Burmese (left) will be well developed and ready for their career on the show bench. This cleverly contrived picture (below) shows a proud father snapping his prizewinning son!

A cat that becomes a Champion can start competing for a further title, that of Grand Champion, which is even more difficult to attain. Neutered cats compete in a similar way for Premier Challenge Certificates and in England three such prizes entitle the cat to the title of Premier. Again, further honours can be won by neutered cats, the title of Grand Premier being much sought after.

Cat Shows for pedigree cats are held all over Britain and in most States of North America. To find out about shows, their dates and venues, it is best to ask the breeder of your kitten for names and addresses to contact. The offices of the Governing Body will also furnish details, usually on receipt of a stamped addressed envelope, and rules for entering shows are despatched with schedules of classes to would-be exhibitors about two months prior to each show.

Most pedigree shows throughout the world are run on basically the same lines. The kitten must be registered, and it is advised that it has been fully inoculated. There are age limits, both upper and lower, and these vary from country to country. Having been registered by its breeder, the kitten must be then officially transferred before exhibition, to the name of its new owner. The show schedule is mailed to new exhibitors on request and contains full instructions for entering, and a copy of the rules of the association or club running the show. These must be strictly adhered to or disqualification may be made after the show and all prizes and entry fees forfeited.

It is probably best to go to your first cat show as a visitor only, and to look around the pens of kittens of the same variety as your own. Chat to the exhibitors; you will find them sympathetic and friendly and often glad to give advice to the novice. You may find that your kitten is not quite up to show standard, but it is still fun to put him into competition just to be sure, and a good way to learn about showing.

With the show schedule, there is enclosed an entry form. This must be filled in very accurately using the kitten's registration certificate to check that the details are correct. Each class has a separate fee, and there is usually a benching fee to pay in addition for the use of his pen all day. The fees must be paid at the time of entry, and the Show Manager will usually help with queries on receipt of a stamped addressed envelope. Be sure to avoid telephoning, if possible, for Show Managers give their time freely and work extremely hard under great pressure, with printing and other deadlines to meet, and the pre-show days can be a very traumatic and tiring time for them.

Having sent in your entry and been accepted, it is up to you to get your kitten in top condition for show day. He should be fed carefully and well, and checked by the vet as regards teeth, coat and freedom from parasites. He should be groomed daily but not too strenuously or his coat may become too thin and sparse. He should be placed in his carrier each day for a few moments, and perhaps taken out in the car in the carrier, to get used to travel without becoming sick. Have visitors to your home pick him up and handle him, and make much of him, then he will handle well at the show and not be frightened of strangers. Buy a cot blanket of some white, man-made fibre, a white toilet tray and white food and water bowls. Make sure his carrier is draught-proof by covering the sides with thick brown paper or plastic if it is made of mesh or wickerwork, and you are ready for the show.

The winners of each breed class, if considered of exceptional merit, are passed before a panel of senior judges (below) and the Best in Show exhibits are selected. The kitten with the most votes is awarded the title and is lifted high by the steward for all to admire (right).

The day before the show is the time to check that everything is ready for an early start the next day. Prepare the carrier with a soft blanket on lots of newspaper, give the kitten an extra careful grooming and clean out his ears. Feed him fairly late so that he gets a good night's sleep. In the morning, give only a very tiny feed and allow the kitten to use his tray, then pack him securely in his carrier. Make sure you have all the items you need for his comfort during the long day ahead and set off, aiming to arrive fairly early at the show hall.

On arrival at the hall, there will probably be a queue of exhibitors with their cats and kittens, waiting for their animals to be examined and passed by the team of veterinary surgeons. They check that the cats and kittens are free from any sign of infectious disease and are not harbouring any form of parasitic infection. After examination, you can take your kitten into the show hall where you will find rows of numbered pens, one of which will correspond to the number your kitten has been allocated.

Clean the pen with a mild disinfectant on a sponge, then place the partly filled litter tray inside. Fold the white blanket into a neat pad next to the tray, then you can take your kitten from his carrier and place him in the pen. Here he will stay all day, and the judges will come to him for assessment of his potential, if this is a British show. In the U.S. and in some other countries, however, stewards take the cats from their own pens and carry them to a judging arena, where they are placed in special judging cages. Then after each class, they're returned to their own pens once more.

Judging goes on most of the day, but at an arranged time, usually to coincide with the admittance of the general public, it is permissible to approach your own kitten and feed and water him, as well as giving him a general tidying and another grooming if necessary. There are award boards in the show hall which give the class numbers and the results of the judges' decisions. These are displayed as each class is completed and the results can be marked down in the official catalogues available to exhibitors at a small fee.

Later in the day the official prize cards and rosettes are affixed to the pens of the winning cats and kittens and the owners of Open Class winners begin to get excited, wondering if their pet has been nominated for the Best in Show awards. Tension mounts as the climax of the show approaches and the selected few exhibits are passed before the expert panels for the final judgment. Most shows have a special array of pens for the top winners and those voted into the highest places are put reverently into the specially draped and garlanded pens. Best Longhair adult, then kitten, then neuter are picked. Then follow the British Shorthairs, then the Foreign Shorthairs, and last the Siamese. Some shows have a non-pedigree section, and the winner joins his more aristocratic cousins in the special Best in Show section.

There are many cat clubs and societies, one of which is certain to cater for your favourite variety, and with luck there will be either a stall run by the club at the show, or alternatively, they will run an advertisement in the show catalogue. Different clubs have slightly different functions. Some are all-breed clubs and run annual cat shows, others are specialist clubs and just cater for a particular breed or variety. Many issue quarterly, half-yearly or annual bulletins or newsletters full of information and amusing articles, and most have social functions at which one can meet others interested in the same breed, or just cats generally. Use your time while waiting for the long judging process to take place in looking round the hall and chatting to the various stall-holders and club secretaries. You will learn a great deal and enjoy your first show enormously.

At the end of the day, you put your kitten back into his carrier and pack up all his belongings. You remove the prize cards and rosettes from his pen for you may take these home with you. At some shows the prize money is given out in the closing stages, at others it is mailed out three or four weeks after the show. The catalogue gives details of how much to expect for each award your kitten has collected, but do not be surprised to find that even if he has done really well, you

91

are likely to be out of pocket for the day. Cat exhibiting is no way to make money!

If your kitten has not won anything at all, do not despair, for the competition may have been fierce, or he may just be at an in-between stage in his development. The judge, once he has finished all his classes will not mind you asking for his honest opinion of your pet, and will point out good and bad faults to you. However, if you bought your kitten from a reputable breeder for show purposes, it is better to contact her for advice. If the kitten was bought as a pet, at a 'pet' price, it is not likely that it will take top honours, but may pick up a few cards occasionally.

Make the journey home as short as possible, for both you and your kitten will be tired. Change your clothes, especially your shoes, as soon as you arrive home, for they may have infection from other exhibits at the show on them. Take your kitten from his carrier and make sure that he has travelled well, then give him a drink and a feed and let him have a much-needed rest. He will probably sleep a lot the following day too, as a first show is quite an experience for a kitten. You will probably feel tired too and it is certain that you will never forget your very first cat show.

The results of the cat shows are often published in various journals and papers. In Britain the official organ of the Governing Council of the Cat Fancy is a bi-weekly publication called *Fur and Feather* in which each judge reports, favourably or otherwise, on the exhibits in his classes and describes just why each animal was placed as it was. These reports are invaluable to breeders, as they can check on their own and other breeders' stock, striving to improve weak points.

In the U.S. and other countries, there are various magazines which give the main show results, and some even award Cat of the Year prizes on a points system. Some countries give huge trophies and wonderfully contrived rosettes instead of prize money, and others just award specially designed certificates. The world over, though, it is the most perfectly formed cat or kitten, shown to perfection, in perfect health and beautifully groomed and presented that will reach the top of the role of honour.

Britain is unique in the world in holding one specialist show on the last Saturday each July. This is the Kensington Kitten and Neuter Cat Club's annual event and, as the title would suggest, is staged only for kittens and for neutered adults. The bulk of the entries are the new season's crop of top breeders' litters and are planned to be born and grow on especially for this show. Obviously, as kittens become cats at nine months of age in Britain, a kitten can only be shown at one Kensington Show, and the quality is high, the top awards hard won. This show acts as a shop window for the breeders, and visitors from all over the world flock to London to see and perhaps buy promising kittens. Most breeds are represented by kittens which are well up to the desired standards of points, and a perfect day is had by all who visit the show because they all have one thing in common – THE LOVE OF KITTENS.

Whether pedigree, like this patchwork Tortie-and-White (below), or just house-pets, like these lovely ginger twins, there is a place in every heart and at most cat shows for kittens of every description.

Index

Acknowledgments

The publishers would like to thank the following organizations and individuals for their kind permission to reproduce the pictures in this book:

Animal Graphics: endpapers, 23, 26, 29, 36 above, 44–45, 48–49, 56, 67, 72; Bavaria Verlag: (O. Kneule) 55, (E. Seeke) 39; Sdeuard Bisserot: 17 above; Bruce Coleman Ltd. (Jane Burton): 50 above; Anne Cumbers: 4–5, 7, 11, 12–13, 14–15, 16 below, 18–19, 20, 21, 24, 25, 27 below, 30–31, 32, 33, 34, 35, 36 centre, 42, 47, 49, 51 below, 54 above, 58, 59 above, 62, 65, 88; Robert Estall (Malcolm Aird): 41; Will Green: 1, 51 above; Robert Hallmann: 38 below, 88–89, 90, 91; Graham Howard: 22; Louise Hughes: 31; Jacana (M. Claye): 76–77, 84–85; (P. d'Ottreppe) 6 below; (Grosse) 75 above; (J. M. Labat) 37, 70–71, 94–95, 96; (Bernard Rebouleau) 63; (G. Trouillet) 52–53; Jane Miller: 57, 60, 61; John Moss: 2–3, 6 above, 9 below, 10 below, 15 above, 17 below, 27 above, 36 below, 38 above, 40, 54 below, 59 above, 68–69, 73, 75 below, 78–79, 80, 81, 82, 83, 86–87; Pictorial Press: 15 below, (Anne Cumbers) 28; Spectrum Colour Library: 8, 74; Tony Stone Associates: 10 above; Sally Anne Thompson: 9 above, 16 above, 19, 22, 43, 46–47, 50 below, 64, 66, 92, 92–93.